A Journey of Wilding Women

Alison Williams
and the
Wilding Women Storytellers

Fritillary Press

Published in 2022 by Fritillary Press

ISBN Paperback: 978-1-7391947-0-3
Ebook: 978-1-7391947-1-0

Published with the help of Indie Authors World

www.indieauthorsworld.com

IndieAuthors
World

Dedication

To WindEagle, whose ageless wisdom and love have made this journey possible.

To Judith Shepherd, wilding woman 1948 – 2022.

Acknowledgements

I owe a huge debt of gratitude to the wonderful wilding women who journey with me, as we continuously co-create our journey through story and images, through conversation, challenge and laughter. These are the wilding women who have taught me the power of generous collaboration, the humility of strength, the discipline of process, and not to take myself too seriously.

First, there are the story tellers, whose tales of their experiences, their hopes and their strengths illuminate these pages with richness and depth:

Tania Watson	Sally Bromley	Cinda Cash Walsh
Carrie Gooch	Catherine Robins	Genevieve Giffiraud
Mary J Oliver	Cedissia About	Soo Young Lee
Shelley Assiter	Sarah Matalon	Karen Chevallier
Leah Marcelline Christensen	Sarah James Wright	Judith Shepherd
Carol Bailey	Wanda Gregory	Alison Wooding
Sophia Jackson	Johanna Steele	Beck Elphinstone

My love and appreciation and deep gratitude for how each of these story tellers have also become wilding sisters, listening with that loving intelligence that helps me hear myself; that helps us to hear ourselves.

Then there are the people of whom it is a truism to say "This book would not have been written without the help and support and love of...." but true nevertheless:

My Teachers WindEagle and RainbowHawk who started me on the Medicine Way in 1999, and have continued to guide me and challenge me ever since. WindEagle has led me through two vision quests and many teaching ceremonies, and her unconditional love and clear far-seeing eye have held me through the depths and heights of walking the Medicine Way; and reminding me always that "Medicine people don't run".

The many women who have given their time and expertise freely and generously, helping to shape the wilding women community, now and into the future, advising on the wilding principles of inclusion and diversity, on running our monthly conversations, helping hone my focus and stay motivated when the journey seemed endless. There are so many – and among them are: Tania Watson, Alison Wooding, Sarah James Wright and Mary J Oliver; and others who kept me up to the mark, and critiqued the drafts: Rose Pipes, Catherine Robins, Soo Young Lee, Carrie Gooch and Shelley Assiter. Then the amazing Cat Brosius: my thanks for building an elegant and clear website – and Wanda Gregory for enabling it – and Karen Chevallier for the Wilding Women logo.

The lovely, enthusiastic and rigorous team at IndieAuthorsWorld for getting this book into shape and into your hands: my editor Aimee Walker, publishing support from Rachel Hessin, design work by Sinclair Macleod, and the indefatigable and unflappable Kim Macleod who guided me through the sticky bits.

Elspeth Maxwell for her intuitive illustrations for the cover and story headings.

The extraordinary people who turned up during the Covid-19 lockdowns with inspiring creative online sessions, especially Eun Me Ahn and Clint Lutes of 1:59.

My children: Max Latey, Theo Shand and wilding woman Clara Speedie Shand, who continuously let me know they are proud of me, and urge me to keep writing and sharing. And my granddaughters who carry the wilding forward with such energy and grace: Annabelle, Colette and Lily, Maebh and Alicia.

And lastly, the two wonderful men who have bookended this process: Iwan Williams who told me I could do whatever I put my mind to, and David Adams, who always knew I could do it. My love and deepest appreciation to them both, and my gratitude to the Universe for sending such extraordinary men to walk with me on my wilding journey.

Contents

journey

jûr'ni, noun

A day's work or travel (obsolete); any travel
From: 13th Century French journée–jour a day, a day's travelling
[Latin diurnus a day's portion]

journey

jûr'ni, collective noun
A company of wilding women

Introduction

It's hard work living in the open in a small tent
with the night temperature below freezing.

I'm bundled up in a down sleeping bag, with a down jacket, a hat, hood and heavy fleece trousers, sometimes I wear my thick gloves as well. The ground I'm pitched on slopes slightly, so over the course of each night I slide slowly and inexorably downhill.

Because I have a bad cold my bladder wakes me up twice, sometimes three times a night, and every time I wake, I have to navigate all the layers. First I have to wrestle with the sleeping bag zip. Why do sleeping bag zips always get caught on the edge of the lining? There's something about my being all scrunched up by the tent door that makes it catch – if I could only get my legs straight it would be easier.

Okay, got the sleeping bag zip down far enough to clamber out of the bag. Next: the tent door zip. Be nice to me, please... This zip is unpredictable – sometimes it unzips smoothly all the way around, result! More often it sticks halfway so the only way out of the tent is to lie on my side, put my head and elbow through the space and do a kind of jackknife wiggle onto the sand and dust of the desert outside. Worst of all is when the zip unzips itself from its track, leaving a gap either side which isn't quite large enough to struggle through. By this time, things are getting urgent.

I force my way out, making it certain that the zip will stick even worse next time.

So, I'm out of the tent (a one-person bivouac) and need to find my shoes. I know I left them just inside the tent where I'd be able to find them easily, but with my overnight slide down the slope they've been buried underneath all those small camping items that seem so important in daylight but are nothing but a nuisance at night. Small clumps of tiny vicious cacti make walking barefoot impossible. Things are now getting seriously urgent.

Found the shoes, abandoned the gloves, working on the layers of clothing... The moonlight is so strong that I don't need my torch, a small blessing. But I do need it for getting back into my tent. If I can find it...

Here I am, a woman in my mid-seventies, mother of three, grandmother of eight (my own three, plus honorary grandmother to my partner's five), five times married (but that's another story), living with Parkinson's disease, completely alone in the high desert of New Mexico on a vision quest. I'm spending five days and nights in solitude and reflection – guided by my teacher – living outside with the temperature below freezing at night and up into the 70s during the day.

My friends tell me – somewhat enviously – that I'm crazy.

They could be right.

But in the morning, waking just before sunrise, getting out of the tent easily – this once – and listening to the coyotes yipping and howling round the plain below me, I am overwhelmed by a sense of happiness so intense it leaves me breathless.

This book is...

This book is a braid with three strands:

The first strand tells the story of my quest in the high desert of New Mexico, how the wilding concept emerged, and how a community of wilding women has grown up around it.

The next strand is made up of wilding stories, written by remarkable women from across the world about their own wilding moments. As they say: 'The stories are beads in a necklace of power'. For some, anonymity gives power. For others, power comes from claiming their story.

The final strand is a set of very practical wilding tools, practices and ideas, each with a challenge, a question, an invitation, to do your own work towards discovering, enhancing and celebrating your own wilding.

This book is a survival guide:

'One day you will tell your story of how you've overcome what you are going through now, and it will become part of someone else's survival guide.' Brené Brown

The wilding stories each carry the seeds of someone's – your? – survival. The powerful themes that run through them are indexed at the back of the book, signposting the stories that are most relevant to you, right now, right this minute, as part of your survival.

This book is a map for our journey beyond survival to thriving, and beyond thriving to living a life of shining, wilding selfhood.

When 'I don't have to make myself small any more'.

CHAPTER ONE

What is wilding?

Sometimes a life shifts. Something happens, something is said, someone arrives or departs and life shifts; it is never again the same. The moment when you see something in your life as it really is, and once it's been seen, it can never be unseen.

These are the wilding moments. They are, as Minna Salami says in her wonderful book *Sensuous Knowledge*: 'realizations from which you can never return, light-bulb moments that shape your destiny.'

Where has wilding come from?

I am in New Mexico to take the next steps on a journey I've been on all my life, telling and retelling my story to myself; looking at myself, my life, my place in the world: opening myself up to the unexpected. And this is the story of how that unexpected happened on my quest, the unexpected idea of wilding, of the wilding moment, of living a wilding life.

I started writing this book with the simple intention of telling this story. But as I wrote, it has also become the story of how the wilding idea developed and grew and became real. It has become the story of how women from across the world came together to explore wilding and deepen our understanding of it: what it is, how it works, what it feels like. It has become the story of how this community of women told their own wilding stories, sharing them with each other, and drawing together the themes and threads that run through them.

We have been exploring how the process of writing our own stories and reading other women's has impacted and changed each of us. As Shelley, one of the wilding women, said, 'Sometimes our story harbours shame, so we keep it inside. By telling the story, we liberate ourselves of the secret. This can have a big positive impact on our lives.'

The first story (originally written in French – you can find the French version at the back of the book), takes us through the writer's experience of one unforgettable Christmas holiday. She tells us about her wilding moment when everything in her life shifted, how she felt, what she then did, and the journey towards a new life for herself and her son.

Happy Christmas

My life dragged on... living as a couple without really being one, my child brought up between us, creating a triangle of attachment despite our friction. For nine years we lived under the same roof, becoming more and more estranged.

The break had to happen, sooner or later. I had just bought a house that needed a lot of work done so I could be independent without necessarily separating. I wanted to test our relationship beyond the day-to-day life that was so undermining us. The split happened during the construction work on the house, on 23rd December.

I was driving with my son to spend Christmas with my family, and my mobile phone rang. Stopped by the side of the road, I listened to my partner screaming that he was throwing all my belongings out of the window, in garbage bags, on the grass, in the rain.

Jealousy and alcohol proved him right: I was to blame, and he was taking revenge. What should I do? Turn around and put my son at the centre of this maelstrom? I called some friends who lived nearby and asked them to get the key for the neighbours' barn from the entrance to our house, pick everything up and stack it in there.

A few days later he said to me, 'You see what you made me do?' I pulled a face on the other end of the phone. He was no longer angry, but sad and worried about what would happen to him in relation to my ten-year-old son. On one point I was very clear: their relationship did not have to suffer because of ours. I would do whatever it took to make sure that it would continue if he felt he wanted it to. He carried on looking after him every Monday evening, since I had just found work three days a week seventy kilometres away.

Having been away for two weeks, I came back early, without my son, to find somewhere to stay – a room, lodgings, some kind of refuge for my son and me. I also went to see the extent of the damage done to my things piled up in the barn: spoilt books, clothes stained with Indian ink, lost jewellery... *Only things*, I thought! I was strangely calm, just preoccupied with planning my future life. A girlfriend offered me a large room with three beds in her attic and I created a welcoming nest with some boxes for clothes, books and toys. We camped there for eight months in this in-between life.

All through this time, helped by a mason/builder, I pushed forward on the work on my house, four days a week, twelve hours a day, my body sometimes in pain, but my spirit free!

During the final summer push a small lake saved me. After days of hard construction work, I would swim, singing my thanks to Oxum, the Afro-Brazilian river goddess, letting my muscles relax with the power of the water and finishing with a salutation to the setting sun.

And on the 31st August, the day before the start of the school year, we were finally living in our own house!

An invitation: Writing your own story

What are your own wilding moments? When has something in
your life changed for ever? When have you just known that you
can never go back to where you were before? What happened,
and what did you feel? What did you do?

This is an invitation to write your own story and think about
sharing it with the wilding women community.

https://www.wildingwomen.com/our-stories

Who is wilding for?

Wilding is for every woman who has – at one time or another – suppressed her wilding self to fit other people's, or society's, expectations; or indeed to fit her own ideas of what she ought to be.

Terrible word, 'ought'. It goes along with 'should' and 'must' and 'need to' – words that are warnings I have slipped off my wilding path and back into trying to be a 'good girl'.

Wilding is for every woman who has stifled her creativity – put off or postponed following her calling. Wilding is for every woman who has succumbed, for a moment or for a lifetime, to Virginia Woolf's *Angel in the House*, the creature who leans over your shoulder as you are writing (or drawing, or composing, or writing code, or thinking for yourself) and whispers gently into your ear, as Woolf wrote about book reviewing in *Professions for Women* in 1942, 'My dear, you are a young woman. You are writing about a book that has been written by a man. Be sympathetic; be tender; flatter; deceive; use all the arts and wiles of our sex. Never let anybody guess that you have a mind of your own.' And for every woman who, as Virginia Woolf said, 'did my best to kill her. [...] She died hard. [...] Killing the Angel in the House was part of the occupation of a woman writer'.

Wilding is for every woman who has feared being called feral, being seen as out of control, unruly, dangerous, hysterical, who has been stopped, or caught, or held back.

Wilding is written for every woman who knows – or wants to discover – how to allow her righteous passion to show up in whatever way it is needed; to speak truth that might be uncomfortable; to listen to, and to hear, what needs to be heard.

The history of wilding women

The wilding concept is not new. A few years ago, killing time before a train journey, I wandered into a charity shop to browse the book section. There on the shelf was a book I had been avoiding for thirty years: Clarissa Pinkola Estés' *Women who Run with the Wolves: Myths and Stories of the Wild Woman Archetype.* It is a powerful book; reading the first chapter I recognised my past experience of coercive control by a now – thankfully – ex-husband. Reading further on I knew that I had to take my artwork seriously, and within two weeks had found and moved into a studio space. Reading on yet further, I found the courage to confront and heal a place of pain between my daughter and myself. Estés' profound knowledge of folk tales from across different cultures illuminates what it is to be a woman; what it is to deal with the pressures and expectations of society; and, most importantly, what it is to identify and tackle (finally!) the internal restrictions that, as women, we so often accept from society and place upon ourselves.

We find wilding in the histories of wise women and healers through the ages and across cultures. In Middle Ages Europe, when so many thousands of women healers and creators were called witches and murdered for proposing alternatives to men's medicine and power, women often hid in plain sight in the convents – Hildegard von Bingen in the eleventh century, Catherine of Siena in the time of the Black Death, and Caterina Vigri in fifteenth century Bologna. The convents themselves had often evolved from the pagan 'colleges' of priestesses, and were, too, a way of well born women remaining single to protect their wealth from the claims of husbands.

We find wilding women in folklore: Morgan le Fay, the Arthurian wise woman and fairy herbalist; the silkie or seal-woman in the myths and fairy tales of different continents and cultures. Wilding is found in women warriors every bit as strong and accomplished as men in the folk tales of

Central Asia, and in Hua Mulan, the warrior-woman in Chinese folklore (although these last stories come with the caveat that it is only socially acceptable for women to be the equal of men if their power and skill benefits at least one of the male characters).

The recent retelling of the Greek myths of Circe, Penelope, and the women of Troy are celebrations of wilding women who move from the edges of the men's stories (Odysseus, Achilles, Hector and the rest) to the centre of their own.

The eighteenth, nineteenth, twentieth and twenty-first century waves of feminism in the Western world have brought us wilding women like Mary Wollstonecraft, Emmeline Pankhurst, Shirley Chisholm, Betty Friedan, Audre Lorde, bell hooks and Rebecca Solnit among so many others – the pioneering women who fought and continue to fight for the right for us all to be seen and treated as fully human equal members of society.

Rewilding nature

We find wilding in the recent ecological wilding and rewilding movement, harnessing the power of nature to rebalance and heal itself after its merciless exploitation by humans. As Michel de Montaigne (Book III 1595) said over four hundred years ago: 'Let us permit nature to have her way. She understands her business better than we do.' Isabella Tree has written with passion and enthusiasm about how she and her husband have rewilded their farming estate of Knepp in Britain, watching with joy as rare species of plants, animals, birds and insects return to their acres, and how the process has made their estate financially viable for the first time.

Rewilding our relationship with nature

The ecological wilding movement looks, too, at how in order to change the future of our countryside we have first to change ourselves. George Monbiot's book *Feral*, his account of what he sees as the devastation in

Scotland and Wales caused by herds of deer and sheep who strip the hills of trees, creating a desert, suggests the reintroduction of wolves. This would, as he acknowledges, require a radical shift of vision and long-held privilege-based attitudes. (I heard it said, not two weeks ago, that the six sea eagles spotted off a particular part of the west coast of Scotland were 'six too many'. No one in our small walking group, however, said anything in agreement – a significant change. The silence that greeted this statement was louder than argument.)

Simon Barnes' *Rewild Yourself* builds on this sense of how we have to change ourselves before we can change anyone, or anything, else. He takes an approach of quiet activism and – seemingly – small ambition; all contributing to a sense of what an individual can do. Wilding in its current Western meaning and context is about a radical transformation in how we as humans view our link with the earth, and how we act towards the earth as a result of that transformation – something central to indigenous societies for millennia. Wilding ourselves is a necessary step towards wilding, rewilding, healing, and restoring our communities, our peoples, our planet, our Mother Earth. In her seminal book, *Finding the Mother Tree*, Suzanne Simard tells her story of having to battle over many decades to establish that trees communicate, cooperate and support each other – her work has helped to reframe how we understand the earth.

Wilding is in the teaching of indigenous peoples in the Americas and Australia and beyond, straddling the cultural divide. Robin Wall Kimmerer weaves academic and indigenous approaches to environmental biology in *Braiding Sweetgrass*; and Leroy Little Bear's work with quantum physicists David Bohm and David Peat explores how the verb-based Blackfoot language, rather than the noun-based languages of English and mathematics, lends itself to understanding and expressing the concepts of quantum physics.

Climate change is a growing and increasingly urgent aspect of the ecological wilding movement. This next very short story is notable for what the author does not say, as much as what she does. When holidaying with friends on Majorca – she refused to fly from the UK – her journey took nearly two days of rail and ferry travel at either end of the holiday.

Finding my environmental voice

*When I left my husband and daughter and
lived alone with my son, I had a car.*

I could not afford to keep it and arranged for it to go back to the work that had had it before. When it was time for me to buy, I had changed and become green, so I never got a car again. I was environmentally aware, as, in my twenties, back in the seventies, I had met an Australian woman. She was aware of the degradation of the world and our need to stop using carbon. I was late to the game in 1995 but have become more and more committed since.

Judith Shepherd

Minna Salami, who we met earlier, suggested an alternative way of being a woman in the world, where the idea of women's knowledge, holistic and handed down over generations, 'brings the non-human natural world in our feminism'.

Breaking away to beautiful

*I am tempted to write about a pivot that makes
for an enticing story with a cheery ending. But
a personal shift isn't about 'happily ever after'.
For me, catharsis manifests through a decisive
movement away from what is no longer working.*

Like pushing off the end of the pool in a swim meet like a shark was at your heels. It is a jolt to break stagnancy, to stop late night bingeing on Korean dramas, to draw out the venom that needs to be spoken and cut the binds of toxic dynamics.

In an undertow of resentment, fights with my husband left me gasping for air. Each time the heat and rage cleared, I felt this keening for my own life that sang out across clouds embracing the moon.

I started biking in the middle of the night, writing while my hands danced uncontrollably and swimming in frigid waters again. Ending the habits that drained me made space for tangible delight.

Lately, I am running toward the wild unknown because only there can I leave behind my shedding skin. Women often believe that we can only leave when there is nothing left of us except dry skin and porous bones. But we forget that we can start anew and find many layers of skin and new beginnings.

Fortunately, death has been whispering in my ear. I have a close friend who just finished a battle with cancer, my mom lost a close friend and Covid-19 is chomping at our heels. All these markers of mortality remind me, 'if not now, when?'

I crave boldness and an untamed heat. That means leaving my marriage, living by the spray of the ocean. That means writing, dancing and gulping down joy in big bites while running where the sand meets the water, dancing in the hushed air between redwood trees.

This is what I know. I need the ocean, big trees and a vibrant community. There is a call to be bigger than security, more expansive than surety. I want love again that is big enough to hold the light bursting from within me.

In a song called 'Wildfire' by SYML, the chorus repeats, 'Sometimes we break so beautiful, and you know that you are not the only one'.

This is what feels broken: a happy
ending for our child to believe
in and regret for the fragile
vulnerability that was shared.

This is what is breaking beautiful:
exploring instead of containment,
risking instead of fearing and
believing rather than doubting.

A beautiful breaking is the
loosening of the limbs. I draw my
palms in toward my heart, spiral
them inward to unfurl out beyond
the body, splay outwards and flap
as if flying, to fly outside the lines
of the familiar.

When I come out of the ocean, my
body sings red, smarting from the
cold. I am alive. My skin and cells
are buzzing in a quiet frenzy. This
is my happy ending.

Wilding now

The wilding concept has existed in one form or another for many thousands of years, but in this context, to me and the other women in this wilding journey, it is a new and exciting discovery. In *The Creative Mind* Margaret Boden suggests there are two kinds of creativity: historical (h-creativity) which changes cultures and history – Newton's theory of gravity, for example, Braque and Picasso's Cubism, Marie Curie's discovery of radioactivity, Ada Lovelace's algorithm that was the foundation of computing science, Galileo's discovery that the earth circles the sun, Shakespeare's writing, Einstein's theory of relativity (alas, so few women come immediately to mind) – things that are done or created or discovered after which nothing can ever be seen in the same way again; and personal (p-creativity) where ideas are generated, new to the generator, without being culturally or historically significant. Like the moment I discovered that if I added the juice of half a lime to a pan of reheated rice with a twist of sea salt the whole dish started to sing; or when I realised I was trapped in a coercive control relationship, and I could live and thrive perfectly well with my child on my own: so I left. None of this is earth-changing, and all of it has been done by others many times before me, but it is the first time I have done it, the first time I have seen it clearly. It may not change the world, but it changes me.

These are my wilding moments, these p- or personal-creativity moments, small or momentous, one-offs or repeated over the years; and they are all, as the wilding women say, 'moments when I grow into myself'.

Years ago I was hosting a group of amateur painters in a session run by a Chinese professor of watercolour painting. He had us making marks on double-spread newspaper with huge brushes. He looked at my wide sweeps of ink, grinned broadly and said, 'You – wild!' It has taken me until now to grow into the realisation of what he could see thirty years ago.

CHAPTER TWO

Who am I?

*We start with a fairy tale I originally wrote
as a thank you to Mick Cooper, an existential
psychotherapist who helped me sort out a load
of old emotional rubbish accumulated over the
years, housekeeping that was in itself a wilding
moment, and cleared the way for yet more.*

At our first meeting Mick asked why I had come to see him. All the many reasons that had brought me into the room vanished from my mind and to my great surprise I found myself saying 'I don't know what I'm called'. Over the course of my life I have had my maiden name, my first married name, my second married name, my third married name and my fourth married name: the one I have kept.

At the start of a conference in Canada in 2000 I introduced myself as Alison Waugh, my maiden name. It is pronounced the Scottish way with a hard 'gh' at the end and I spoke about the difficulties this gave me. In England people pronounced it Wawh (and asked if I was related to Evelyn Waugh); in France I was Voe; in Italy, Wanghi; but boarding my Air Canada flight for Halifax, I was greeted by the cabin crew, 'Good morning, Ms Wow!' That, I told the conference, is who I will be for the next few days. And by the end of those few days, I had met and fallen in love with the man who was to become my fourth, my late, husband. Wow! Indeed.

My fifth life partner and I committed joyfully to each other in a wedding ceremony with our teacher, WindEagle, some years ago.

Fairy stories should be heard. If you are reading this one on your own, out of earshot of other people, then read it out loud. If you are with other people, and prefer not to disturb them, then read it at speaking pace under your breath. Let your lips move. The rhythm of a fairy tale is like the rhythm of casting a spell; one of the oldest incantations in the world is: 'Once upon a time...'

Once upon a time, long ago and far away, there lived a young woman.

This was no ordinary young woman, for she was made of mirrors and glass that sparkled and shone in the sun. Everybody loved the young woman, for with her brightness she was very beautiful, and with her mirrors she reflected everything that was wanted of her. She had the magical gift of giving each person exactly their heart's desire.

But inside the sparkling mirrors and the shining glass, the young woman was very very small, much too little to carry the mirrors' weight.

'I am so tired,' she said. 'Whenever someone wants me to be this person, then someone else wants me to be that person, and another one wants me to be another person, and it just goes on and on until there is nothing left of me except the mirrors and glass, and they are so very heavy to bear.'

And the young woman sat down and wept. And as she wept her tears ran down the mirrors and the glass.

And the years passed, and the young woman grew older and still she wept. And she had three beautiful children and still she wept. And those children had children and still she wept and still her tears ran down the mirrors and the glass.

But this was no ordinary woman. Each of her tears held a tiny drop of magical joy that wore away at the mirrors and the glass. And the more the woman wept, the greater the transformation.

And then wise people came who looked through the glass and the mirrors, and a most curious thing came to pass – the mirrors and the glass started to dissolve in her tears. They became thinner and thinner and weighed less and less.

And then another most curious thing came to pass – the thinner the mirrors became, the taller the woman grew. And the lighter the glass became, the stronger the woman grew, until the mirrors and the glass were like gossamer and the woman was tall and strong.

Then the woman stood up, and dried her tears, and laughed a great shout of laughter. And the last of the mirrors and the last of the glass shattered and was blown into nothingness.

And the woman stretched out her hands to the world, stepped out onto the path, and walked away laughing.

The end.

Or rather, a beginning.

Who am I? Who are you?

My knowledge of who I am, my understanding of who I am, has shifted and deepened over the course of this wilding women journey, through writing this book, through my own wilding journey and my connection with the journeys of the women I have been walking with.

Before wilding women I asked myself: Who am I? Mother? Wife? Friend? Academic? Writer? Patient? Person with Parkinson's? Artist? All of these and more? By the end of writing this book, I begin to have an inkling...

An invitation: Who are you?

How many hats do you wear? How many do you wear at the same time? Visiting my mother and stepfather at Christmas was a nightmare. If I was trying to be a good wife, then I was probably being a poor daughter. If I was managing to be a good daughter, then I was usually seen as being an unsupportive sister, and so on.

Selfhood is knowing who I am and taking who I am – ME – into every situation. When I am myself, then it doesn't matter what role I find myself expected to play. I am me, capable of being a great mother, a competent and supportive work colleague, an inspiring friend, a loving and surprising grandmother.

When was last time you found yourself caught and conflicted by other people's expectations of you? Expectations that didn't match what you felt about the situation?

Make some notes about it – the situation, the conflicting expectations other people had. Just writing it down will help you see things a bit clearer. This will be your touchstone, a reminder you can return to every so often on this journey.

CHAPTER THREE

Starting my journey

It is said there are only two possible plots for any story: a stranger comes to town or you go on a journey. This story, my wilding story, starts with the first and moves into the second.

Teachers

The strangers, RainbowHawk and WindEagle, came to town, to Edinburgh, late last century. Carriers of ancient wisdom, this extraordinary couple were bringing an ancient body of self-knowledge and earth wisdom to people across the world, sharing their gentle, strict and deep ways of living and being. In vigorous middle age, dressed for the extremes – heat and cold – of the New Mexico high desert in intricate handwoven garments (I can hardly call them anything as prosaic as clothes), RainbowHawk's long white hair braided and WindEagle's free-flowing, they walked into my world and my life shifted.

They became my teachers, and over the next twenty years I learned – and am still learning – about the old ways of living, the ceremonies of indigenous American cultures.

In the first ceremony I attended in 1999, I discovered what it meant to be seen, completely and non-judgementally, by another person. I had to leave the ceremony early, and as I nervously approached RainbowHawk to make my apologies he saw me and thanked me for coming. In that moment I knew that my presence in the ceremony had been, for him and for the ceremony, significant. I felt completely accepted as being the best of myself, and at the same time it was unsettling to catch a glimpse of that best and be challenged to grow and deepen it.

RainbowHawk died – transitioned – in 2012, and WindEagle continues their work. Knowing RainbowHawk was – and still is, as he turns up in my dreams and my inner voice – a delight and always a challenge. In my last dream about him I was pontificating about a new concept of creativity I had written out; RainbowHawk looked at it, looked at me, and said 'Yada, yada, yada – just DO it!' Challenge indeed.

And here I am, about to embark on my quest, sitting on my own in the desert, just DOING it.

The quest

I am looking out across the plain to Pedernal, a mountain of the Jemez range, sacred to the Pueblo First Nations. The October sun is warm on my back and the wind has the keen edge of the sub-zero nights. A hawk slices diagonally across the fierce blue New Mexico sky and pinyon jays dip for cover in the juniper scrub. There is a venerable pinyon pine behind me, and I am held in a silence made only deeper by the wind in the pine needles, the last of the cicadas chirruping – and my total solitude.

The path to this moment, here on the land in New Mexico, has wound through the joys of connection and love; the sorrows of loss and bereavement; through ceremonies and teachings; learning and forgetting; making and crafting; and through two quests in the high desert.

I dithered for a long time about the first quest – the time, the cost, the travel, the emotional commitment – and finally I asked David, my dear friend and life partner, 'why should I go?'

'Because it matters,' he said.

I went.

Running through this story is the thread – acknowledged and honoured – of my physical state. Six months before my first quest I was diagnosed with Parkinson's disease. In the high altitude of New Mexico and the experience of living joyfully in the moment, my condition hardly impinged at all (anecdotally, people with Parkinson's respond well to altitude). Indeed, if it hadn't been for having to take my medication at prescribed times, I would have forgotten about it altogether. But it is an inescapable fact of my life, and my energies and time are bounded by it, and doubly precious.

This next story is written in beautifully idiosyncratic English by a French wilding woman.

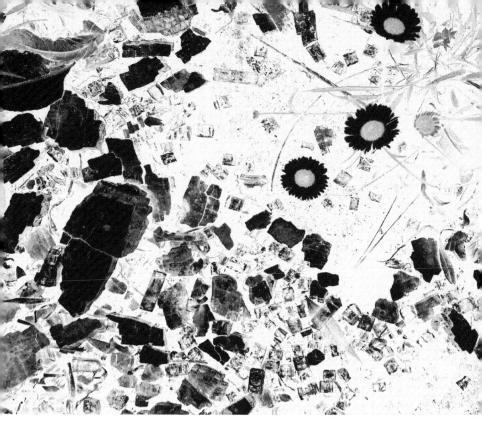

Wilding woman

*Once upon a time a sixty-year-old woman
learned she has a degenerative neurological
disease without any hope to recover.*

No, it is not a fairy tale but a nightmare because this old woman is me.

From that time, I tried to know the psychic reason of this disease through introspection. And I discovered that all my life I have not paid attention to me. I was who other people want me to be, and their opinion mattered to me.

After reviewing what was my life before, I realised that my life was so interesting, hectic, at that time I was always running, but after what?

Just in a hurry, a woman in a shell, without emotions, just « DO ». It was a life compliant to this very materialistic system.

And I understood that this meant my soul said 'stop' through my body.

AND SO WHAT?

Little by little, my priorities changed.

For example, I never heard birds singing in my garden. I never saw how the mountains were beautiful from my windows.

Would there be something else I never understood?

Yes of course, nature: the trees I speak to now, animals whose language I understand and feel their energy. Dancing, singing, all these crazy things!

And I saw that I belonged to the universe, not only to the human.

That is how I became a wilding woman.

Very few people understand my evolution. The others say, you have changed, we don't recognise you. What is happening? Are you ill?

This is the price to pay for me, to have become a wilding woman. And I regret nothing.

New friends, new life, and I have never been so happy to be a wilding woman.

And now I AM at seventy years old! Never too late.

A quest, as I experience it, is structured with great care. A month beforehand, I am required to do deep preparation – time in nature thinking and feeling through questions: Why the quest? What has brought me to it? What is my innermost desire for it? Once I arrive on the land in New Mexico, a day and night camping on the land with the other seekers, tasked with listening to the land and discovering the messages it has for me. Then into solitude, in a bounded space, living on the Mother Earth for five days and nights, food and water brought each evening. And each day my guide coming to sit for a time, to direct, to listen, to challenge. And throughout the quest, a task set.

An invitation: What is your heart's desire?

What is your heart's desire? If you knew what it was, what would you do?

In the previous story the writer talks about it never being too late at seventy years old, to live the kind of life she wants, to hear the birds singing, to see the mountains, to speak to nature...

She was determined to stop being 'in a hurry, a woman in a shell, without emotions, just DO, always running, but after what?'

What would you stop doing?

Quest preparation day

First, my preparation day. There is a seashore some way outside Edinburgh (where I live) whose long curving beach is backed by dunes, sandflats, salt marsh, and Scots pine woodland. A river cuts across it, banks overgrown with yellow flag irises and meadowsweet, and the sandflats and the salt marsh are alive with birds, wildflowers and insects. The woodland paths are soft underfoot with many seasons' depth of pine needles, and dragonflies and butterflies hang suspended in the sunlight filtering through the branches. A few minutes' walk from the bus stop, it is where I choose to spend my quest preparation time. My task is to be with the Mother Earth for a day, listening to what she has to tell me about the what, and why, of my quest. Then to write a letter for my teacher, telling of my intention, of my commitment and purpose.

I walk from the bus stop towards the sea, rucksack with picnic, journal and waterproof trousers and jacket borrowed from David (the September weather is unpredictable) slung over my shoulders, alongside the river, across the sandflats, over the dunes and onto the beach.

I'm just being. Letting the paths lead me, following my curiosity, opening my mind to everything, quieting the internal chatter. Noticing...

Tasting life on land and sea

Golden light is pushing through the round windows. Playing in the sunbeams are 'wishing stars' (dust renamed by my toddler) that eventually land on the menagerie of fish tanks.

Peering in, I see a blue Siamese fish swimming sideways. Red and blue tetras are floating to the top. The larger fish are nipping at the smaller ones. One tank is so dark with algae that the fish are only visible as green shadows. With trembling hands, I sprinkle the food flakes as an angelfish leaps and bites my finger.

This has happened to me a hundred times. These nightmares come to me when I have neglected my inner life too long.

At the beginning of our travels, mornings began with solitude by the campfire. While sipping tea, I read tales about retrieving my wild pelt and how to enter turbulent waters like child's play. Narratives sprang forth from my limbs that wanted to be danced. While watching the coals burn red, ideas materialised to unravel with words and images.

This ritual was halted when a red sun cast a sepia tone to our shores. The smoke from the fires was so close that it impaired our vision. Days were spent trying to manage our exposure to the bad air. Then the fish dreams appeared to remind me of my hunger for solace and solitude.

Anais Nin wrote, 'We write to taste life twice, in the moment and in retrospect.' But even before writing, reflecting in quiet helps me make meaning of what has been lived.

Late in the evening, I entered into the cove of my inner world. Playing with recent memories, I could see that the octopus has been a burning symbol. My toddler is obsessed with them. We marvel at their ability to be fierce, soft and adaptable. Before getting out of bed, we act out skits of bad crabs being eaten by octopus, good jellyfish befriending an octopus, baby octopus fighting baby shark, etc. We see octopods everywhere – in kites, beaded trinkets, made with sand and seaweed, and in a moving documentary.

This cephalopod spends a lot of time alone without family. Their survival depends on their ability to camouflage, seek refuge and build a slow trust. When they lose a limb, it grows back and becomes fully functional again. Savvy octopods have been known to eat sharks and some of them can walk in both worlds of the ocean and land.

As an edge-stalker, I want to swim in the air and walk in the water. This magic can only happen when I seek my own time and shade in the kelp forest. This means I keep running along the beaches and let the frigid waters wake me from my complacency. I can begin anew after I cut off the vestiges of my failed relationship.

After diving in repeatedly inward, I see my thriving is dependent on an intentional seclusion to find meaning in the wondrous encounters in my life.

Noticing: The birds

The birds are with me all day. From the bus window I see two buzzards soaring and hunting over the fields. I can't hear the high mewing sound they will be making, but I know it is there. Onto the sandflats and small wagtails scurry about, tails flicking continuously up and down. The skylarks, alarmed by my approach, start up from the ground, rising 'on long thin strings of singing' as Alastair Reid's poem *Scotland* has it. They fly as children's kites do, dipping and regaining height before tumbling to the ground. The gannets' hunting flight is very different. There must be a shoal of fish just off the shore because there are six, maybe ten (impossible to count at this distance) gannets diving. They fly to a great height, then fold their wings and plummet headfirst into the sea with a plume of white water splash, surfacing shortly after. They are elegant, mesmerising, deadly.

On the shoreline the young gulls are noisily harassing their parents for food, being for the most part ignored – the young are now full-sized, and only distinguishable from their parents by the mottled brown of their plumage. The message: you are old enough to fend for yourself, is not getting through. A flight of oyster catchers, the jetfighters of the seashore, rocket their way deafeningly along the beach. A single cormorant, black against the water, sails gracefully across the waves. And from somewhere, unseen, a curlew spills its liquid, haunting, soul-reviving song.

The woods are full of woodpigeons.

Noticing: Colour and wildflowers

The whole place is rich in colour and flowers and insects.

The waves are everything from faded celadon to Homer's 'wine-dark sea'. The dry sand is pale silver, the wet, a dark gold. On the salt-flat there is a bushy ground creeper covered in cream flowers, alive with all kinds of bumble bees and worker bees. White bladder campion, yarrow, deep purple-blue vetch and yellow bird's-foot trefoil. Purple-pink rosebay willowherb. The delicate purple-blue of the thyme flowers. Marron grass. A very small bright green grasshopper skips out from under my feet and into the grass by the path. And a big black beetle. Bright sunlight, strong wind – sand skittering along the surface of the beach.

I had hoped to walk from the beach to the woodland to the west but found that the beach tapered into a long spit of land separated from the opposite shore by a deep, fast-flowing river, so I had to turn back. The sand caught my feet, and the wind blew it, stinging, into my face. I trudged slowly back along the beach, head down, feet dragging, tired and getting hungrier by the minute.

But even in my increasing fed-up-ness – made even more uncomfortable by the awareness that the day and the walk and everything I do today are held in ceremony, and feeling that maybe fed-up-ness isn't supposed to be part of it – I am diverted by the way the sand skims along the surface of the beach in the same kind of snaking, curving lines you get by zigzagging a skipping rope or a garden hose across the ground. My eldest son, a physicist by training, once explained to me the physics of why dust collects in corners. I'm sure he would know why sand blows across the beach in these snake-like patterns. I make a mental note to ask him when next we speak (I forget).

Off the beach and heading towards shelter (it is threatening rain), it is the insects and the flowers that keep me going. I know the names of many wildflowers from my childhood, seen on family picnics, and on the camping holidays that were the start of my respect and love for the land, for nature, for Mother Earth. My parents named the flowers so easily and casually that I learned without ever feeling that I was being taught. It is somehow a courtesy, knowing the names of the plants I spend time with, in the same way it is courtesy to know and remember the names of people I spent time with. In her book *Gathering Moss*, Robin Wall Kimmerer says much the same: 'In indigenous ways of knowing, all beings are recognised as non-human persons, and all have their own names. It is a sign of respect to call a being by its name, and a sign of disrespect to ignore it. Words and names are the ways we humans build relationship, not only with each other, but also with plants.' One of Hilaire Belloc's poems starts:

> Of courtesy it is much less/Than courage of heart or holiness/
> Yet in my walks it seems to me/That the grace of God is in courtesy.

The continuity of sheep

STORY 6

After visiting my friend in Glasgow Infirmary, I board the train for Penzance. Gaze out of the grubby wet window. It's raining.

The train accelerates. The sky clears. I see sheep grazing on the Moffat Hills. It occurs to me they'll graze long after my friend dies. Long after I die. This makes me happy.

Nabakov says existence is a crack of light between two eternities of darkness. It's not.

Walking on a Scottish hillside years ago with a good friend I stopped to point out a clump of lady's bedstraw. My friend had been brought up in London where, as she said, 'there are roses and then there are daisies, and everything else is just weeds'. She told me many years later that that was the moment she realised that all plants had names – and she now gardens with passion and intelligence, creating spaces of great beauty, and tucked in behind her shed a small potager where she grows potatoes, courgettes, beans, tomatoes, and raspberries, rhubarb, gooseberries, red- and blackcurrants and more.

Connecting with the land

My relationship with nature, with the land, runs deep. My aunt told me that when she wheeled me in my pram she would pause under the trees. She loved seeing my eyes dancing as I watched the leaves catching the sunlight and shimmering in the wind.

When I was three I was sitting on the draining board with my feet dangling in the kitchen sink, the sun streaming through the window picking out the fine blond hairs on my legs. 'Mummy, mummy, come quick!' I called. 'My legs has growed little flowers!'

Both my parents were teachers, so all through my childhood we had long family summer camping holidays that nurtured and deepened my connection with the land. This connection has informed my artwork, as I notice and absorb the structures and shapes of plants as well as their names, knowing their uses as well as their habitat.

Foraging

Foraging – food for free, as Richard Mabey's book calls it – has always been a pleasure. On a very low-budget student trip through Italy, I gathered wild sage to tuck into the slices of bread and cheese that were all we could afford. They became a feast. On another journey wild thyme and marjoram spiced up the tomato-and-tinned-tuna messes we cooked up for ourselves. Toiling up a steep Scottish hillside, I found a second wind when a friend gave me wild sorrel leaves to chew. Their sharp lemony taste stung and refreshed. I discovered how using my teeth to strip the pith from inside rushes and chewing it made saliva flow again to a parched mouth when I hadn't brought enough water on a long walk. Plain lettuce became salad with wild sorrel and wild garlic leaves added; and discovering the hair-thin stalks of wild asparagus growing by the roadside on a Majorcan holiday was a triumph of taste and thrift.

Each autumn, when I lived in Scotland's Highland Perthshire, my children and I would hunt for chanterelles, looking under beech trees where they seemed to like to grow. The trick was to harvest the largest and leave the others – the littlest ones and the ones past their prime – to shed spores for the next year's growth. Fried in butter with garlic – and with wild garlic leaves chopped into the pan at the last minute – they are quite wonderful. As are puffballs, white and firm enough to be tossed in garlic and butter, before they go over and become white balls of black spores that explode into the wind when you squeeze them.

I always thought that field mushrooms had to be gathered early in the morning because of taste, or tradition. Nothing of the kind, said my pragmatic American friend, Nancy. You harvest them early before anyone else does, and before the flies get to them. That way you don't have to pick the maggots out of them. She was quite right. Gathering field mushrooms can be frustrating – they are the same colour as scraps of shed sheep's fleece, and I have crossed fields many times only to find that I could gather enough wool to spin a hank, but not a mushroom to be seen. Scottish countryside walks are a treasure hunt for blaeberries and perfumed wild white raspberries, wild strawberries, brambles.

I go foraging in the city as well as in the countryside. The best, biggest, sweetest brambles I know grow in a tiny wild corner of an Edinburgh suburb – or did until the corner was tidied up. In garden hedges and parks, young spring leaves are tasty – the early hawthorn we called spring salad, and – discovered from my horticultural daughter-in-law – very new lime leaves are delicious although the texture can be on the slimy side. A treat is finding sweet cicely, a cow parsley whose leaves smell of aniseed when crushed, and whose seedpods go from an unripe soft green you can eat, snacking as you walk, to a hard oily brown-black that – so I'm told – yields a fragrant furniture polish when crushed. The seedpods can be infused in warm milk, making aromatic custards. This plant in particular comes with a health warning – most of the cow parsleys are poisonous, so if you are not sure whether you have the right plant, leave it alone. As with all of these harvestings, if in doubt: DON'T.

My first father-in-law was in a German prisoner of war camp during the Second World War and told me how the French soldiers ate so much better than the British. The French made salads from wild herbs, dandelion leaves blanched under cloths, wild garlic, and caught and bred snails for protein and taste. They were altogether healthier and better fed than their British fellow-prisoners who waited for their Red Cross parcels to augment the meagre rations they were served. (Along with another British officer, he escaped and made it to Spain, and hence back to Britain. Sitting by the dockside in Spain with his fellow escapee waiting for news of a ship, a bomb exploded, killing his friend, but knocking a fire pail off its fixings upside down over his head and so saving him, at the cost of the hearing in one ear.)

Being with the earth, listening to the wind, hearing the messages

But I digress... back to my preparation walk, and I look at the journal entries I wrote:

> The children's play park with its benches and tables is quiet; I eat my picnic there.

Walking again. Ominous clouds, so I make my way towards the woodland.

Into the woodland with dragonflies, butterflies and a jay. Cool Scots pines.
Muscles aching from walking and from the weight of the rucksack.

The threatening rain blows off and I find a spot overlooking the dunes, in the sunshine and sheltered from the wind. In my journal again:

Head on my rucksack, I sleep in the way one does in the open air, aware
of the wind and the birdsong, of the heat of the sun, aware of turning over
impressions and thoughts in my mind. And still deeply asleep. When I wake,
my aching muscles are beautifully eased and my preparation thoughts
beginning to emerge.

There is a bench looking out over the estuary, and as I find it the rain sweeps in very cold and heavy, so I put on my waterproof trousers and David's jacket. Warm and dry and insulated, I sit gazing at the horizon, watching the way the rain blows across the landscape in patterns much as the sand blew across the beach. Intermittent gusts sweep it into shapes and layers, building an exquisite beauty.

On the sand someone has written D – A – V – I – D in stones.

A huge wind all day.

When I get home, I write my letter of intention. I structure my thinking round the suggested headings; the day has done its work – the messages from my connections with the earth flow out.

I write:

Here is my quest ceremony preparation letter, sent with love and deep
intent...

I talk of my yearning for this quest, a yearning that has been growing for over two years, and of my sense of excitement – what is the next extraordinary gift/insight that I will work towards?

I express my wonder at the health I have been gifted, and my determination to use it wisely and well – where should I focus? I talk of my sense of time passing. And the need to choose, to choose wisely, where I put my focus, not simply to react to circumstances.

I reflect on my Parkinson's and that I have a choice about how I live. I write:

> *I choose to live fully, richly, generously, and to act as if the disease is negligible. And at the same time, to quote Robin Morgan, 'I am not diminished by my Parkinson's, I am distilled by it. And I really like the woman I am distilling into.' I want to get to know this woman completely.*

I acknowledge my gift of making art, and the dawning realisation that my work is good, and I must honour it.

And finally, responding to: 'What is my deepest question?'

> *To find, and live, and live in, my elderhood – how do I do this, deepen this, live this day by day by day? How do I use the time and energy and gifts that I have, for good, for the people, for Mother Earth, for my close and loved ones? To quote Hannah Gadsby, 'What is the purpose of my Human?'*

For some years now I have held the idea of elderhood. I see it as a state of balance, in which I have the knowledge and emotional resources to react appropriately to whatever occurs. As Rollo May says, 'Sanity lies in the pause between stimulus... and response.' I watch my teacher and notice how she will take a calm breath before she replies to a request, or responds to something she hears or observes. On the first day of my quest, I ask her about the stick I have requested to help me find my feet on the uneven ground. I'm tired and my bad cold is getting worse, and I ask in what my mother would have called a bratty way. She looks at me, pauses, and silently hands me her own stick. I know that this stick is precious to her – it belonged to her partner – and in that moment I see quite clearly that I don't need it, that I have indeed been a brat, and that she knows that I know, and that it is all right – another moment of learning. For the rest of the morning, I guard the stick zealously and gratefully hand it back the first moment I can.

Re-reading my letter now, I realise that elderhood is, for me, wilding. Living in elderhood is living in touch with my wilding self, in my wilding space, on my wilding path. No wonder elderhood has felt so elusive all these years – it wasn't rising up from deep inside me. Instead it was a lack, not a joyful seeking. This process of writing, revisiting, relooking and remembering is powerful. And it is this process that will underpin how the wilding stories are written.

I sent my letter to my teacher, and the reply came: I am being held in preparation for my quest. It feels right.

This next story is by a wilding woman who was undertaking her quest at the same time I was doing my first one.

Be still

I entered a five-day quest with two others in New Mexico, with a sacred woman guide. It was the first time in my life that I was completely alone, in a limited space chosen by myself, given limited food but water always available. No iPhone, books, watches, etc. were allowed, only a journal and writing items. My guide would visit me in the morning providing guidance if I chose to follow it. In the evening, she would bring food that was to last until the following evening. Essentially, I was on my own living in a tent.

The first day prior to finding my space, my guide had a series of very small scrolls with sayings on them; we each picked one at random. Mine read:

Beloved North, Breath of All Life.

We call on your power and presence in respect and with love.

May the winds of change, of healing and awakening blow sweetly and gently in the hearts, minds and bodies of All Beings everywhere,

That we may all expand and awaken to our highest potential,

In concert with all of life in the Me Song.

The day before the week ended my guide said that sometimes Questers sense an expanded identity being born within them. I said I'd think about it. Later that night the words: WindSong came to me. I immediately said, 'No, No, No' out loud. I didn't want that name because I had vacationed in Bermuda many years before with a couple whose husband treated me badly. The name of the house where we stayed was WindSong, and I had bad memories about the experience and didn't want anything to do with that name.

Later that night as I sat looking into the darkness, I saw the extraordinary brightness of the North Star... the star that has guided my ancestors throughout thousands of years. I then remembered the randomly chosen message on the scroll from the first day that ended, 'In concert with all of life in the Me Song'. And I knew that my expanded identity and expanded name was WindSong.

My guide's question to me upon leaving my quest: 'How are you going to live as WindSong?'

The following year I began another programme with leaders schooled in the teachings. It ran over two years with regular week-long retreats – indoors and outdoors – when we had guided projects and a lot of 'alone activity' time.

At one of the early retreats, I laughingly said to one of my leaders that I felt something in me was 'cookin'' but I didn't know what.

The following day, I suddenly felt emotionally vulnerable, weepy, teary eyed and wanting to cry. We were each asked to meet with one of the leaders to debrief our learning so far and I chose one. As I sat with her, I began to sob uncontrollably. As I finally spoke, I said to her, 'I don't know how much more beauty I can take.' After a long pause, she said, 'I don't know either, but it sure is f***in' beautiful.'

Coming in contact with 'beauty' was profound, deep, soulful and transformational. I felt that I had expanded, awakened my Being on my planet Earth and feeling more closely connected to humanity. I felt more conscious of my life and the world around me, and I felt alive differently.

Then I was asked to stand in all four directions: east, north, west and south for a period of time and then to 'be still', to see what might happen. I was sceptical about doing this – what could just facing four different directions do? I felt silly. But I did it anyway; and I then remembered the first sentence of the poem that Maya Angelou wrote when Nelson Mandela died to commemorate his life. Her poem is called *His Day Is Done* and the first sentence is, 'The news came on the wings of a wind, reluctant to carry its burden.' That sentence is so extremely beautiful and meaningful to me. And, at that moment I used it as a basis for my own poem written as WindSong:

> *A breeze came on the wings of Universal Oneness.*
>
> *A Gathering she said.*
>
> *Come with me to see as I see; every heartbeat, every breath, full of beauty, light*
>
> *and life.*
>
> *Fear nothing, love is the answer.*
>
> *The song of serenity, tenderness, comfort and acceptance sings a soulful refrain –*
>
> *Be Still, it is here.*
>
> *Be Still, it is here.*
>
> *Be Still, it is here.*
>
> *Be Still, it is here.*
>
> *It is in you now, and forever.*
>
> *Cinda Cash Walsh*

An invitation: What do you already know?

It can be difficult thinking through what to do, making sense of our jumble of thoughts and feelings. Wilding is finding out what we already know deep down inside.

Spending time in nature, time with Mother Earth, helps unravel the thoughts. When you simply stay in the moment, noticing what is around you – birds, colours, sensations, plants and animals – some kind of pattern emerges and begins to make sense.

Try it – give yourself a day, or an hour, or five minutes, to be in nature, with nature. Find a field, a park, a garden, a beach, or a single tree, and simply listen to whatever comes.

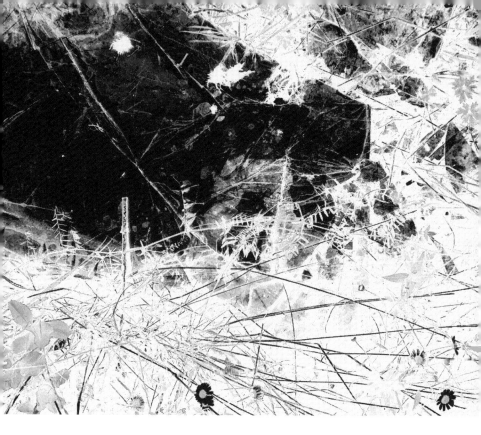

My marvellous year

Being uncertain about the meaning of 'wilding women' and unsure, too, that whatever it might mean, I may well not be one of them, I decided instead to write about my marvellous year, the year when I awoke and the world was wonderful, full of endless possibilities. It is a time which remains vivid in my memory.

It was 1963; I was nineteen and had left school the previous Christmas, having sat the Oxbridge entrance exams and gained a place to go to Newnham College, Cambridge, the following October. That was already rather marvellous, if slightly alarming. I had nine months to earn money and maybe have some fun in what would now be called a 'gap year'. So I got a job delivering the Christmas post, which was what students in my generation did every year, then worked on the floor packing tea in J. Lyons' tea factory until I landed a plumb job in the milkshake bar at the Ideal Home Exhibition in Olympia. This was when it all started.

Also working in the milkshake bar, with its jersey cow in a stall, was Christine, a girl I had not met before although she lived near to me, who came to be, and still is all these years later, my best and dearest friend. We had a great time making milkshakes during the day and racketing around with other young people in the evenings. All rather tame in today's terms, but enormously exciting then.

Sometime during that month, Christine and I decided we would spend the summer travelling to Greece and hitchhiking round the Peloponnese to visit the legendary sites of ancient Greece. This was, for us, an enormous adventure since at that time, there were no cheap flights and such a journey was by train from Calais to Paris, making a mad dash across the city to catch another train heading south. It was a Graham Greene sort of journey, taking three whole days and nights, with numerous train and station changes and regular checks of our tickets and passports from border guards as we crossed from one country to another. One memorable and slightly scary moment during this uncomfortable journey, was when we reached what was then communist Yugoslavia, and the border guard who came in the early hours of the morning to examine our papers was distinctly not amused by two foreign girls with virtually no luggage and travelling alone. However, the moment passed and finally we arrived in Athens, travel soiled but full of anticipation.

This, of course, was Greece before the Colonels' coup and before the advent of mass tourism.

The following two months were a dream of wonders with some distinctly hair-raising moments. We stayed in youth hostels, eating scarcely anything except yoghurt and cucumbers with the odd hard-boiled egg, and agreed that if only we had as much as ten shillings (old money) a day, we could have afforded at least one good meal. Still, it didn't seem to matter as the sun shone, we were a novelty act as we hitched round the peninsular and people were almost universally kind, even though we spoke not a word of Greek.

There were so many wonders to recall; some which stand out were walking down to the Lion's Gate at Mycenae, standing alone with no other human beings in sight in the temple at Delphi, visiting the palace of Knossos on Crete, the theatre at Epidaurus, the battlefield at Marathon. It was a blessed time, but it had its challenges and hitchhiking provided some of them,

most notably two rather dashing young(ish) men who drove a white Citroen DS, then a legendary and stunning car, and who pursued us round the Peloponnese, even on one occasion bribing the youth hostel warden at Delphi so that we had to barricade ourselves inside our room; we were the only visitors to the hostel that night.

Like all times of dreams, our Odyssey finally came to an end when Christine departed for a visit to Germany and I to a month as a monitrice in a colonie de vacances near Dijon.

This, then, for me was the year in which I was awakened to so many possibilities, a magical year, a time of splendour.

As I finish this short piece, I have received via Facebook a photo of my daughter-in-law, Peggotty, wild water swimming down a freezing river on Dartmoor with her sister-in-law. This, I think is truly what it means to be wilding women.

CHAPTER FOUR

Into the quest

The quest land takes my breath away. It is like nothing I have ever seen before. Red rocks, ochre dust and sand and tumbleweeds, deep green pine trees and juniper scrub, vivid yellow cactus flowers, and above it all a sky of a blue so sharp you could cut your finger on it.

Being with the land

The strong earth-palette colours unsettle my northern ideas about the traditional primaries of red, yellow and blue. When I was pregnant with my youngest child, I found that I couldn't read my daughter her favourite bedtime story; the illustrations' colours, these same colours – deep earth red, yellow ochre and pine green – made me nauseous. We put the book away until my younger son was born, and then brought it out afterward, queasiness gone. It is startling to find myself in the middle of a landscape whose colours affect me viscerally. This time there is no nausea, instead an elation at the strangeness and beauty of the place and a paradoxical feeling of homecoming.

Moments of aliveness

The land is bordered on the west by a deep canyon dropping almost sheer to a river winding slowly and lazily through stands of cottonwood trees. To the east, the land slopes gently away from the top of the canyon down to a shallow escarpment that sits above the Abiquiu plain and looks across to

67

the sacred mountain Pedernal. The rocks at the top of the canyon are worn smooth by rivers disappeared hundreds of millions of years ago – I play stepping stones on them, reaching from one to the next, pretending the sand is water, as it had once been.

The boulders remind me of the Scottish ones where my brother and I played as children, and that I played on with my own children when they were little, leaping from one to the next to get across a mountain burn (Scots for a small stream) without getting our feet wet, dodging each other's splashings. In his book, *The Atom of Delight*, Neil Gunn talks of 'coming across himself' sitting on a flat rock in the middle of a burn in the summer sunshine, intensely aware of being in the moment, all his senses (and there are so many more than just Aristotle's five) alive and awake.

My mother spoke of such a moment, her 'atom of delight', in her garden in the sun with my father and a close friend. They were sat round a small simple table, painted with falu röd färg or hus röd paint – the deep earth red of so many Swedish houses – brought back from a Swedish camping holiday. They were drinking sherry, and the sun was catching the liquid and casting golden light and clear shadows across the red. On the table lay a single deep indigo-blue gentian. As the three of them sat in contented and loving silence, a bumble bee circled the table once, twice, landed, and slowly and solemnly crawled into the gentian. My quest is rich with such moments.

Here, as in Scotland, there are outcroppings of rock that with a shift of imagination become a horse's head, or a turtle, or a great whale sticking out of the cliffs. There are tiny plants and delicate black fungi (as well as the spiny cacti) growing in the sand, and by using the rocks as stepping stones I avoid treading on them. Across the canyon, the opposite wall is striped earth red, ochre yellow and white as the rock layers change. I realise that the red rocks are the falu röd färg of the Swedish houses.

The land is covered with juniper scrub and pinyon pines, and growing among the small vicious cacti are straggling clumps of tough grasses. To my unpractised eye, each part of the land looks very much like the next and it is easy to lose my way. There is the up and down of the slope of the land, but I have to find markers – a twisted tree stump or a particular set of rocks – to stay on track. Remembering my Girl Guide pathfinding skills, I create small heaps of stones that mark the way. I become better at reading the terrain.

Meeting my quest circle

Once my quest begins, I will be staying on just one piece of land. I will claim the space and protect its borders by ceremonially sprinkling sacred tobacco round the perimeter. Tobacco is powerful. On my first quest, sitting at the top of my site, I became aware of a man waving to me from the lower edge, a tripod over his shoulder and all hung about with cameras. As I said nothing, he shouted: 'are there any petroglyphs there?' Still I said nothing, and he made as if to walk up the slope towards me, then hesitated, turned, and walked away, unable to cross the line of sacred tobacco.

There was an old tree stump at the tobacco line just beside the path to the site. My guide would stop there, waiting to be invited in. 'Ho Seeker! Approaching your circle!' The tree stump became my guardian.

My second site, ten paces by eight, has another guardian tree at the point where the path crosses my boundary. My guide and the helpers bringing food and water each evening all halt well before the boundary and await my invitation.

My second quest – the one in this story – took place six years after my first. I had found myself yearning for a second one, needing time to take stock of my life, to deepen my learning, and to think through how best to use my energies and time wisely and generously. I had a strong sense that this was the time that needed to be seized; and writing this now, in light of the Covid-19 pandemic, I bless the learning that taught me to listen to my interior voice.

So in 2019 I flew to Albuquerque, and then, with nine other quest seekers, arrived at the land where the quest would take place.

Which is where this part of the story starts.

Meeting my quest teachers: Grandmother Tree and Pedernal

My quest site looks over the plain towards Pedernal, the sacred mountain. My guide has introduced me to Grandmother Tree, a pinyon pine of great strength and beauty growing in the centre of my space. I have hung sacred objects on her branches – a bead necklace brought by David from New Mexico on his last quest, a prayer pouch I made, a prayer stick, and messages received the previous day from the land (I will speak more about this later). I watch the birds, insects and lizards as they move across the sand; I listen to the birdsong, the cicadas and the faint rustling the wind makes across the juniper scrub.

Pedernal has requested that I sit with her for the time of my quest: such an honour, such a blessing. When my guide tells me, I weep. In this story, mountains and trees, birds and insects, plants and the earth and stones speak to me.

My quest task

I have been set a task: to reflect on my life as a garden, finding inspiration and learning in the trees and stones, the birds and animals that let me share their space.

At the start of the quest there is a moment when I turn to look back up the path that is taking me to where I will hold my quest. This is the moment when I say goodbye to my life up to this moment in time, when I step away from everything up to then. I am overwhelmed by grief and longing – it is difficult to turn my back on all the familiar joys and sorrows of my life. These are things I know and am comfortable with.

I honour the moment; I honour the life that has brought me to this moment and turn my back on it. I have – without yet knowing it – stepped onto the wilding path.

Here I am then, sitting on the edge of the escarpment, talking to Pedernal, sacred mountain.

I find myself asking her, 'Why did you want me here?' In my mind, Pedernal answers 'Because you are a remarkable woman, and it is time to know it, accept it and get on with it.'

Mountains don't mince their words.

She tells me Grandmother Tree holds the answers, holds the learning, holds the love. She tells me it is time to learn how to live with the grace of understanding that I am remarkable. And to live with grace, holding that understanding.

From my journal, speaking to Pedernal:

I hear you telling me, every time I look at you, that I am a remarkable woman; that I am remarkable.

I tell my guide all this. She says, 'yes.'

Creating my quest circle

In Grandmother Tree's shade I have created a stone altar and have found stones of appreciation to set on it.

Twenty stones, my guide said, each one appreciating a special aspect of myself.

So far there is:

- a red stone, for my capacity to love, to hold and to cradle;

- a blue stone of imagination and dreams;

- a blue and white stone for perseverance;

- a glowing translucent brown-and-cream-and-blue-grey stone for depths both hidden and open;

- a big, mottled stone with an orangey-brown back for my sense of fun;

- a sharp white stone for a sword that cuts through nonsense, seeing clear and true;

- a small-edged white stone – very sharp – for my art making and sculpting;

- a dark-blue rectangular stone with two white edges for my ability to see beyond the expected;

- a small rectangular mottled stone for making connections and leaps of meaning;

- a white flake for friendships;

- a blue flake for cooking amazing food, and

- another for hosting gatherings with meaning, holding and transformation;

- a big rough tough stone for grandmothering;

- others for stillness, for beauty;

- and balanced on top of the fun stone, one for my sense of the ridiculous.

Still, not twenty.

While gathering them, I find a perfectly worked chert arrowhead, a thing of great beauty and rarity. It will be part of the prayers. This land was part of the chert-bearing land held in common by the indigenous peoples from the neighbouring pueblos. They worked the stone for arrowheads, axes and other tools – things needed by everyone, a gift from the land.

Through all this, blessed bird song.

Appreciating my specialness, acknowledging that I have wonderful qualities, does not come easily. A lifetime of modesty, of not putting myself forward, of living with the tall-poppy syndrome (it's the tall poppies that get their heads knocked off) makes it difficult to tell myself: *Yes, I am special; yes, I can help people laugh and have fun; yes, I grow and nourish friendships; and make amazing art, and beautiful meals, and safe and trusted gatherings and spaces.*

Finding objects to represent the special aspects of myself makes it easier. Much easier than saying the words out loud.

At home I have a small corner on the top of my chest of drawers where I put objects that remind me of the best of myself. I see it every morning, and every evening. And I know if I'm getting out of synch with myself if I realise that a few days have passed without me acknowledging it, recognising my own worth.

Time to slow down, time to honour myself.

An invitation: Honouring the best of yourself

Your next challenge is to find things that represent the best, the special parts, of yourself.

If you can, gather the objects from nature – stones, twigs, a beautiful leaf – let your eye be caught by whatever is there.

Or perhaps you have a collection of beads or buttons and can choose the shape, the colour, the texture, that suggest the different aspects of yourself.

Or perhaps you tear out pictures from magazines and newspapers and collage them.

Then honour them – yourself – by creating an altar to put them on.

Have fun with this – it is serious, but not solemn.

CHAPTER FIVE

My life as a garden

Time to tackle my task, to reflect on my life as a garden. I am sitting under Grandmother Tree, asking myself 'What is in my garden? Who is in my garden here and now?'

On the front of my notebook, I write

Quest Garden 2019

I make a list:

- Grandmother Tree;

- A resin-rock, large and triangular, covered with drops of resin falling from Grandmother Tree's branches. Some new and clear and catching the light; some older and opaque, creamy-coloured;

- Three sloping flat rocks under Grandmother Tree, fitting into each other;

- A lizard-log, home to two grey-brown lizards playing back and forth on the log and scooting across the sand to the juniper tree on the other side of the sand patch;

- Butterflies – some white, some yellow, some deep browny-black;

- Birds – ravens, pinyon jays, a woodpecker, LBJs (stands for 'little brown job' – catch-all term for any small unidentified bird);

- Insects – flies, including a large scary-looking one. Two days later I see a praying mantis.

I draw a map of my garden space. On it are:

- Grandmother Tree;

- Juniper bushes (various);

- The rocks mentioned above, including my altar stone;

- Lizard-log ditto;

- A tumble weed;

- My tiny bivouac tent.

And I start to meditate on myself and my life as a garden.

Garden...

I write:

> *Accepting what is there, looking for meaningful relationship.*

> *Garden....*

All I can think about is how, for me, 'garden' carries too many shoulds/ oughts/musts. Weeding. In my journal I write:

> *Garden for me means changing things, bringing hard-won order and 'better than' to it. I think about the gardens my mother created – wonderful temporal sculptures, worked on daily. With places to sit out of the wind ('sit-oot-eries' in Scots), with an abundance of wild strawberries and imaginative plantings, with places for my sculptures and wonderful stones gathered from hillsides, demolished churches and rivers.*

And I am resisting the guilt of gardens...

My journal again:

> *Myself as a garden felt – feels – restrictive, managed, needing constant weeding, keeping off the grass (Virginia Woolf's encounter with the Beadle),*

*and sweeping leaves, howking moss from the lawn, and getting dock and
dandelion roots up from between flagstones, breaking my fingernails as I do.*

*One of the Rothschilds is said to have remarked: 'No garden, however small,
should be without its two acres of rough woodland.'*

It sometimes seems to me that my life has, metaphorically, been a series of
gardens I have created for other people. The garden I should have or could
have created for myself and for my children, inviting others into it – or
not – didn't get started until I was in my fifties. And the default position
of creating gardens for and at the behest of other people is still there, still
strong. I wouldn't mind, but they just enjoy the garden, and don't help
with weeding or maintaining it. So I smile and weed, and smile and dig,
and smile and harvest, and smile and cook, and when I neglect the garden,
out of resentment, or fatigue, or trying to do something for me and the
people I love – Wham! Here's the guilt again. I write:

I'M DONE WITH GARDENS. I have a strong sense of NOT GARDEN.

A sickly sweet Victorian song goes through my mind:

> In my little garden there are roses
>
> In my garden there are violets too
>
> In my little garden there is sunshine
>
> In my little garden there is –
>
> You.

I talk to Grandmother Tree. I am struck by how her roots hold strong and
solid onto the ground. I can't dig down more than an inch or two of soil
before I hit rock – putting in tent pegs is difficult. Her canopy is gloriously
even and balanced, reflecting the spread of her roots.

There is a calm about Grandmother Tree, a complete acceptance of the
other lives that go on in her shade; on the ground around her, and in her
branches. Grandmother Tree IS. She is where and what she is. People,

animals, birds, insects, all life comes to her. Other trees, plants, grasses, sit around and below her and her branches.

And me.

She is grace.

My wilding moment

I sit with my thoughts on gardens, mull them over, sleep on it – or rather, doze in my chair in Grandmother Tree's shade. I doze and dream, and wake with the juniper tree nudging my arm. From nowhere – or everywhere – comes the word WILDING. I come wide awake.

Picking up my notebook, and with more than a little 'So there!' I write on the cover:

My Quest Wilding Place

This is my task: to create and explore the wilding place of me.

This is where I start discovering my wilding self, finding and walking my wilding path.

With joy. On my terms.

My life shifts.

My guide arrives: 'Ho Seeker! Approaching your circle!' And I invite her across the boundary, past the Guardian Tree. I tell her what has happened, how the wilding idea has arrived, how it is itself a wilding moment, how it feels – how I feel – touched by grace.

This is important, she says, women need this; you must write about it.

And so, this book is born.

The next two stories, both by the same woman, are powerful explorations of wilding choices.

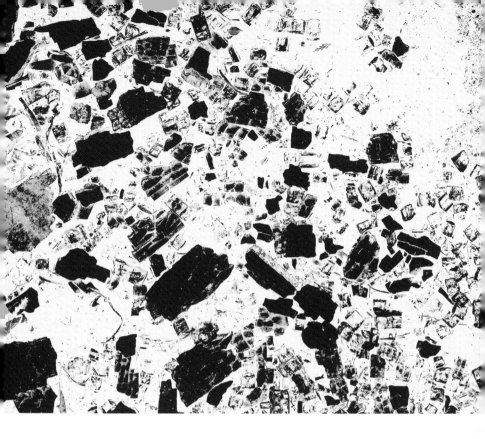

A journey into the night

My search for authenticity, for who I am, has been there all through my rebellion against my restricting upbringing. I was brought up in a traditional Jewish family, which left very little space for questioning and choice. I was blowing with the wind, defying rules and forever searching for what felt me. I was getting lost in the rebellion - it became the aim itself.

I became a mother in 1973, which fulfilled a deep sense of yearning I had. My whole sense of being was about making it OK for the children, smoothing out the rough ride whichever way I could. This meant I was not leading the cart; I was merely pulling it the best way I could.

I found myself with a daughter of five and a baby boy, no money, no support and in a crumbling squat with no electricity and a leaking roof. The solution came in the form of the glamour of night life. I could be with my kids during the day and be the mother I wanted to be. When night came, I was transforming myself into a glamour girl and went out there to serve on rich people's tables – listening to their drunken stories and offering solace and a lot of champagne.

I was pulling out of an abusive, volatile and unhappy marriage; I had lost my voice, my sense of identity and my self-respect. In an odd way, these encounters with those strange men gave me the confidence to tap into what I have always been good at – listening and giving counsel. On a more basic

80

level, I was feeling desired by them, I felt alive. I was allowing the sexual woman to regain her power, I was reclaiming my self-confidence.

This lasted nearly ten years. I was able to improve our lifestyle no end and offer a decent life to my kids. However, there was a high price to pay: the price of a double life and the incongruence I felt with being a Feminist. Nightlife became a trap; it was not a place I could grow older in; it had no future for me. I did not know how to get out and start afresh.

Those were the times of sexual liberation, but I know now how that served men and how oppressed we were as women. By telling my story now, I am giving 'that woman' her rightful place as a courageous, willful and strong woman.

Lilith, the archetype I identify with – the Mother Goddess of childbirth, children, women and sexuality – is also a dark Moon Goddess. She is considered beautiful and dangerous. I want to carry her with pride. I am unleashing her from her hiding; I am dancing with her.

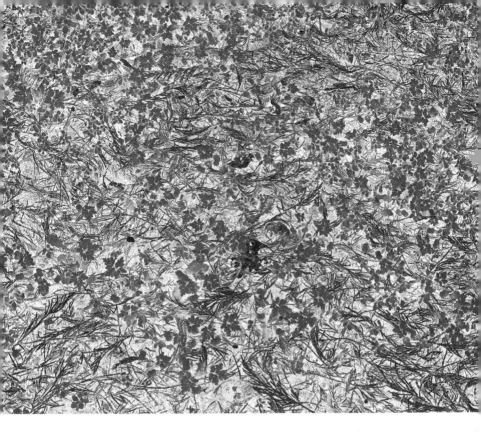

A new dawn

*My mother passed away in 1989. This was a deep
turning point for me. Although my life choices took
me away from her, I always felt that deep mother-
daughter connection. She was a precious soul
with a very good heart. She had also been a rebel
in her youth - defying her strictly religious father's
wishes by becoming a Zionist and immigrating
to Israel from Poland. She escaped the Holocaust
that way. I knew her death was an end of an era
for me and hopefully the beginning of another.*

It was at that time that I started to have therapy and grappled with my demons. I resisted strongly any interference with who I was. The strong willed and stubborn woman held on to her tough grounds. But, some light started to be shed on my confusion and I was awoken to the inner adventure of self-discovery.

Years of training as a counsellor and a psychotherapist, prepared me to start knocking on the establishment's doors, asking to be let in. This was a most painful experience. I was not wanted. I had been on the fringe of society for way too long. I had nothing to show for myself, as they saw it.

This coincided with the birth of my grandson. I felt unprepared – I did not feel 'old enough'. I was so immersed in my efforts to be accepted somewhere, to forge my professional self, that I was not able to offer my daughter the support she needed. My daughter's birthing and my own 'birthing' conflicted. I saw myself as selfish, I felt I was betraying the mother in me and abandoning my daughter, but felt I had to follow my path.

Today, I am a well-established psychotherapist. I completed my master's degree, despite the odds of demanding work commitments. My journey of self-exploration and professional development is continuing. I love what I do. I can look back at that time of my life as one of the hardest mountains to climb. I felt trapped in the nightlife environment. I knew it was a dead end. The struggle to break out was immense. I was terrified I would not be able to change my lifestyle, to fit into society and to make ends meet.

These are two pivotal episodes on the continuum of my life. So where is the little rebellious girl, the woman who pushed through the obstacles with tenacity? I know she is still there, questioning everything, being true to her convictions, her passion, her sense of integrity and humanity. She is no longer a rebel without a cause, blowing in the wind. She is grounded, planted strongly in the earth, like a plant growing uncultivated in the wild, the plant which escaped the conformity of cultivation, which nature would return to its natural being – wild, diverse and whole. For me, it is about reclaiming who I am, returning to the true me.

An invitation: Your wilding moments

Have you started to think about your wilding moments?

Are you ready to write them down? If you are still unsure which wilding moment to write about (we all have many), then go for a walk. The Romans talked about solvitur ambulando or: it is solved by walking. Walking frees up the imagination.

CHAPTER SIX

Mapping the wilding territory

*Sitting in the shade of Grandmother Tree, the breeze
rustling her pine needles, my guide and I talk about
wilding. Her questions are sharp and loving: What
is wilding? What does it mean to live in grace, to be
in grace? What are you yearning for?*

What is wilding? Finding out

I hold the questions. What do I mean when I say I yearn to touch the grace
inside me; to find the Wilding Place within me?

The driving question when I was writing my PhD dissertation (I embarked
on a PhD in my early sixties) was always 'Whaddaya mean by that?' And
when I didn't have a clear answer, I was told to do the work and come back
when I did. Somehow I hadn't expected to be challenged in the same way
on a quest, but when I talk to Pedernal, the mountain, about this – about
my yearning to touch the wilding part of me, the wilding IS-ness of me, the
wilding me – Pedernal looks me in the eye and tells me not to duck it.

Tells me to go back to Grandmother Tree and do some deep learning.
Discover what wilding is, what it means, how it is lived.

I'm an artist; I use mark-making to explore the world and figure out my
place in it. In my studio I paint and draw and make three-dimensional
work. When I am thinking something through, I turn to my notebook – I
write and scribble-think with images and doodles. When I need to go deep
inside myself – to touch my creative unconscious – I often embroider.

85

So my instinct is to reach for my sketchbook and start drawing. My guide
has introduced me to Grandmother Tree, and she to me, telling me I have
much to learn from her. What do I notice? Observe? Hear? And what
do my observations teach me? In my art practice I know that drawing
something allows me to begin to see it with clarity, and not until I see it
clearly do I start to understand it.

'I hear, I forget; I see, I remember; I do, I understand.'

So I draw Grandmother Tree.

I stand below her with my back to her trunk and look upwards, drawing
the branches as they grow out one above the other. Then I move round,
still with my back to the trunk, and draw the next set of branches, and
again, and again, until I am back where I started, and my drawing is
complete. It isn't easy – the bark is scratchy, the ground uneven with roots
and tipping stones, small low branches snag my hair and my jacket, the
wind drops dust into my eyes as I look upwards, and my neck is cricked.

In my journal I write:

> *Finding my path through the branches is difficult – it needs attention. I*
> *make mistakes and they evolve into something else.*

In my journal again, later:

> *I stood beneath this real tree – a pinyon pine – in New Mexico and looked*
> *up. My back against the trunk, I drew the branches as they grew out from*
> *it. Capturing the layers was difficult as the higher branches often followed*
> *the angle of the lower ones, then divided and subdivided in fractal patterns,*
> *each smaller segment the image of the larger. Moving around the trunk,*
> *still looking up, the next main branches crossed the previous, and the upper*
> *branches in that segment fractalled too. The drawing became convoluted and*
> *confused – or rather, I did – as branch grew above branch, thinning with*
> *each repetition. I grew dizzy and stopped.*

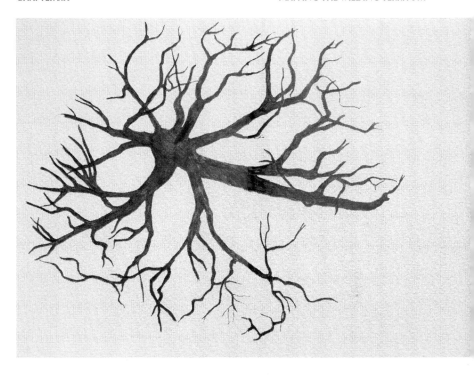

So many of our thought processes happen below the level of consciousness. We're just not aware of them. Guy Claxton in *Hare Brain, Tortoise Mind* talks about the intelligent unconscious – I think of it as my creative unconscious. This is what happens when I 'sleep on it', when I put the issue/problem/challenge to one side and do something completely different to let my brain get on with its work uninterrupted. Sometimes I wake with the answer clear in my mind; sometimes I have to give it a nudge – this is when I will make marks on paper. Drawing, in particular, helps me to free up what is trying to get out, to communicate.

An invitation: Saying hullo to your creative unconscious

What's your way of tapping into your intelligent unconscious?

Do you make marks: scribble-think? Doodle? Mind-map?

Do you make music? Sing? Drum?

Do you write? Jot things down? Make notes?

Do you dance?

Do you go to sleep?

Experiment with different ways of tapping into your creative unconscious: try out some of these suggestions.

Starting to discover my wilding self

I look at the drawing I've made of Grandmother Tree. I see three
concentric rings – the solidity of the central trunk, the comparative
simplicity of the main branches, and the complicated network of the
smaller branches and twigs. I can feel my mind working on this, slow and
just beyond reach. If I try to capture it, the thought will vanish. If I trust
it, the thought will appear when it is ready.

The sun casts deep shadows, giving me shade to sit under, moving as
the sun moves. Then I realise that Grandmother Tree's shadow also has
three rings: the innermost cast by her trunk, the next ring cast by the
main branches, and the outer ring cast by the small branches, twigs and
clusters of pine needles. With my notebook on the ground, I draw round
the shadows cast onto the pages. I draw the shadows cast by Grandmother
Tree on the side of my tent. I sit under her and draw the sprigs of pine
needles at the end of her branches.

I scribble-think, drawing and doodling in my notebook, allowing my mind
to move in time with my pencil, and my pencil to meander with my mind.

What if...

What if... the inner ring, the shadow of the trunk, is my BEING – the
innermost core of me – strong, grounded, rooted, remarkable.

What if... the shadow of the main branches, the next ring, is my LOVING
– my family, my passions, my husband-lover, my art, my friendships.

What if... the outermost ring of shadow, the small branches and twigs, is
my DOING – activities that make up my day-to-day life; the things I do to
nurture and express my being and my loving.

The slow depths of my mind, my creative unconscious, work on this, just
beyond reach. Virginia Woolf described how an idea came to her while
sitting by a river, daydreaming: 'Thought – to call it by a prouder name

than it deserved – had let its line down into the stream. It swayed, minute after minute, hither and thither among the reflections and the weeds, letting the water lift it and sink it, until – you know the little tug – the sudden conglomeration of an idea at the end of one's line: and then the cautious hauling of it in, and the careful laying of it out?'

I am content to wait.

At night Grandmother Tree's shadows are very different from the day shadows. There is a full moon and in its light the shadows are powerful. I write: *The moon is casting strong inky dark shadows.* I wake in the night and walk on my quest land and see there is only one huge moon-shadow pattern, where everything – trees, land, my wilding place, even, I feel, my life – merges into a single shape. Shadows cast by the sun are made up of many small details and different intensities from pale to dark. The moon, on the other hand, casts one single immense fringed shadow that swallows the details totally. Profound black shadow and clear silver light – no half measures.

The shadow holds everything. It fuses the shadows of Grandmother Tree, the juniper bushes, my tent, the smaller plants; and I wonder if this is how my community is made? How everything, still separate, nevertheless merges under the moon?

Writing this, I realise that this is where the idea of the wilding women stories begins, here in the desert, under the full moon. Each story a part of the whole, and the whole strengthened by each individual; the magical connections between so many disparate lives, the threads that weave the greater story together, that co-create a community. In her book, *Braiding Sweetgrass*, Robin Wall Kimmerer talks about how the indigenous Americans – she is of Potawatomi origin – plant corn, beans and squash together. Called the three sisters, the corn grows tall and strong, providing support for the beans. The beans twine around the corn, and trap nitrogen in the soil to nourish all, and the squash spreads around the base, keeping out the weeds and insects. There is a direct analogy with telling this story: the straight, strong central narrative of my quest is the corn. This gives a framework, a scaffolding, that supports the beans – the wilding women stories twining around the central narrative, seeding the ground – the context, the readers' imaginations – with nourishment. The squash is women meeting up each month on Zoom, talking, sharing, learning the wilding practice that sustains themselves and their sisters through the stresses of daily living.

Each day I write in my journal. Each day I welcome and invite my guide into my space, and we sit a while in silence, in conversation, in challenge, in learning and in loving appreciation.

There is a wonderful pattern emerging from my seeing, my observations. It flows around and between:

Being, loving, doing – being, loving, doing...

Mapping my wilding

My guide brings me a white deerskin of stunning beauty. On it I am to create a map of my wilding, of this new territory that is opening up. I know I want to chart the three rings – Being, Loving, Doing – so with string, a needle and a pencil I improvise a compass and draw the circles on the leather with great care.

She brings me paints and ink; she brings me ribbons, threads and scissors. In anticipation I had brought embroidery silks, needles and a silver thimble. I have a large black plastic board and clothes pegs to hold the leather in place.

I wake the next morning having dreamed what to do next. My journal says:

So I do.

I take the skin with its three carefully drawn concentric circles and lay it on the ground. I load one of the larger paintbrushes with dense black ink and flick it hard three times at the white leather. Huge spots of black splash diagonally across the deerskin. Doing it is exhilarating and scary at the same time – ink splashes are usually mistakes, damage. I have no idea what they are, or why they are so important, just that they are, and they need to be there, moving across the skin.

As I work on the deerskin over the following days, I realise the splashes mark the path across the unfamiliar territory of my wilding. They are desire lines – the informal trails created by people walking from one place to another, wearing paths as they go. My ink splashes grow in importance, getting stronger as the map expands, and as I too become more familiar with my wilding territory.

Day by day I work on the wilding map. Day by day it reveals more to me about me, about my wilding, about the wilding process and thinking, being and doing.

'Lasso the moon,' my teacher had said during my first quest. 'The rope is your path.' In my journal then I had written: *What is my path?*

Now, six years later, I am answering my own question.

Step 2

I started attending Al-Anon [for people who have been affected by someone else's drinking] in 2006 and learning about 12-step recovery. Step 2 of the 12 Steps is: 'Came to believe that a power greater than ourselves could restore us to sanity' and Step 3 is: 'Made a decision to turn our will and our lives over to the care of God as we understood him.' Given that I had been brought up by parents who had a strong Christian faith and have always been a church goer, sometimes more regular than others, I considered myself totally au fait with the whole God business and didn't give it another thought.

However one evening I heard a woman sharing on the subject of 'God': she suggested jotting down a list of attributes describing the God of my understanding. I scribbled down the first words that came to mind: all powerful, judgmental, remote, condescending, patriarchal, and unsatisfiable. We were then told to turn the page over and write a list of attributes we would choose for God: I wrote loving, kind, understanding, forgiving, generous, enveloping, soft and yes, womanly. The whole exercise took less than five minutes, but it was real light-bulb moment for me.

Why on earth had I been giving internalised head and heart space all these years to such a negative force when there was absolutely no reason to do so? What a piece of craziness. After all, we're talking about something that can be no more verified than an invisible friend.

It was such a simple exercise but so powerful. Having clocked this piece of nonsense I had been carrying all these years, it was such a joy to be free of it. And I have stayed free, and the now God of my Understanding has joy in all creation including my own craziness.

Exploring my wilding

Each day my guide comes and we sit together. It has taken me years to understand my relationship with her. She is my teacher, Holder of the Ancient Wisdom, and I have been more than a little overawed and tentative. She has waited patiently while I found the balance between deference and respect, admiration and reverence. It is rare to meet someone who knows so surely and unobtrusively who they are, who likes themselves and who is full of love and compassion for others. And who holds herself, at one and the same time, with gentle dignity and an inner strength and passion. She conducted the marriage ceremony for David and me, and over its two days not a single one of the many grandchildren and friends' children cried or fussed. And she can giggle like no one else I know.

We sit in silence, holding unspoken conversations. She asks questions that go straight to the heart of things. There is ancient wisdom saying: 'The first people had questions and they were free. The second people had answers and they were enslaved.'

Each day I work on the skin. There is power in sewing, in the craft and practice of stitching. Clare Hunter, in her wonderful book *Threads of Life*, says:

'Needlework takes time. [It has] to be carefully done. The needle lingers and the stitcher is forced to pause from time to time to re-thread a needle, pick out and cut a new piece of thread, decide what to embroider next, what colour or stitch to use. It allows space for reminiscing, for remembering.'

Needlework also allows space for meditation, and for my unconscious to work on the observations I have made. Each mark I make is an active meditation. Each puzzle – what mark is right? what stitch next? what colour, what paint, what needle, what ribbon, what thread? – explores the nature of wilding. How I live, and could live, within it and by it.

At the centre of the map is the drawing of Grandmother Tree, her branches stretching across the three circles. Clusters of pine needles sit in the middle ring, inside a thin ring of embroidered cross stitch and chain stitch. The whole image is held in an outer circle of shadow forms – the shadows cast by Grandmother Tree in the moonlight.

The map works in me as I sleep – I wake in the middle of the night and see the moon shadows and feel the brace of the freezing air, and know what the map needs – demands – next.

I write it down, so as not to forget in the next dreaming.

Each day, moment by moment, the map grows deeper and stronger. Grandmother Tree's branches I leave as untouched white leather. The inner circle I paint a strong vibrant yellow, capturing the New Mexico sun and the yellow cactus flowers. The middle circle is the deep earth red of the rocks here that glow in the sun against the intense blue of the sky. I embroider rings of yellow and black stitches between the painted yellow and the earth red, and add long streaks of golden yellow and pale green silk thread. I sew a red silk cord round the inner circle.

I work until dusk prevents working any longer, and I sit with Pedernal and watch the colours fade from the land and the sky. I eat, then sleep. Waking in the pre-dawn, I stand and listen to the coyotes calling in the clear frosted air. I watch the growing light bathing Pedernal gently and slowly until the sun rises into the sky, and I salute the new day with thanks and gratitude to my teachers: to the sun, to Pedernal, to the Earth, to Grandmother Tree, and the moon, for their holding, their teachings and their love. Thanks for my teacher and the helpers who bring my food and water each evening.

As I eat my breakfast with slow care and great attention, the urgencies of the map-making rise quietly inside me. I set my camp to rights, re-hang my sacred objects on Grandmother Tree, become fully present and then – into the map-making.

The wilding map grows. There are times when I try to make it go in directions it doesn't want, especially if I try to make the images 'designed'. So I have to unpick the stitching, or adjust the paint colour, or make sense of a rogue line. I have a strong urge to cut out some of the shadow shapes and let the black of the plastic board show through. So I do, and sew the cut-out leather pieces around the edge to become part of the shadow cluster.

An invitation: More conversations with your creative unconscious

Scribble-thinking is a wonderful way of connecting with our creative unconscious. Get a notebook – preferably blank, not lined – and a good set of fibre-tip coloured pens. Let your hand choose a colour, any colour, and without looking at the paper, make marks – any marks – and then have a look at what you have done.

More on wilding...

As the map grows, so does my understanding of what wilding is for me.

In my journal I write:

Wilding is conversations with the Earth, with trees and plants, with rocks and mountains, with sacred Perdernal, with Grandmother Tree;

Wilding is my pathfinding, my walking at ease through the territories of my life;

Wilding is my deep roots into the Earth, my growth up into the branches;

Wilding is climbing the trees, is looking up into the branches, is leaning against the trunk, is treading delicately among the cacti, the fungi, the little plants;

Wilding is the clear path of the moon, the deep tree-shadows she casts;

Wilding is paradox: being purposefully still, energetically quiet, unmovingly moving;

Wilding is listening – even if I have to lose my voice to do so;

Wilding is being at home with myself;

Wilding is remembering. Remembering all this, being true to all this, holding it simply;

Wilding is being in and of my wilding, being on my wilding path, being myself.

I remember a quotation from the 20th century Finnish painter Helene Schjerfbeck: 'Dreaming does not suit me. To work, to live through work, that is my path.'

In my journal, later:

This is a map of a real place;

It is a map of a real experience;

It is a map of a real future;

It is a map of a real now.

This is a map of a real experience – my quest on the land. Each day's experience and learning is in the map: what happened, what I learned, what revealed itself to me. There are moments of insight, moments of huge joy, moments of weeping and of being cradled by the earth.

Later:

It took another two months after getting home to complete the map. The urgency I had felt on the land was still with me – to work each day on the leather. I had an enamelled Victorian biscuit tin full of exquisite, narrow, multi-faceted jet beads that had belonged to my own grandmother, my mother's mother; for many years I had kept them, knowing that one day they would find their place. I had once or twice almost given them away, but something – the small voice, my instinct – had told me to keep them. I sewed them into place, gleaming black rays of sun and shadow.

I had a large sweetie tin full of beads and beading needles. Given to me a few months ago, I hadn't known until now what I would use them for. They found a place on the work –as if they had been gifted especially for this, and I am sure that they were. I laid the leather out on the floor and scattered the beads in handfuls across it, sewing them where they fell. They became the shining parts of the path, illuminating the dark ink, swaying freely in loops and strings. Some of the beads were magnetic and clumped together on the pathway like the black fungus on the land in New Mexico.

I found heavy black felt and stitched the leather map to it, edging it with tiny black beads, so small that no one notices them until the light catches them and they shine, black upon black. But I know they are there, and that is enough.

And, forgetting until now what my teacher had said, I sewed a large round disc of mottled stone – the moon – onto the black background at just the point where the path leaves the leather and travels on and out into the night.

I had indeed lassoed the moon.

Wilding questions

What is wilding? What does it mean to live in grace, to be in grace? What are you yearning for?

I hold the questions. What do I mean when I say I yearn to touch the grace inside me; to find the wilding place within me?

Listening for the small voice

Part of wilding is learning to listen for, to hear, and pay attention to our small voice. And to believe and trust it. I kept the beads.

My small voice knows huge things as well as little things.

The first time I was aware of hearing my small voice was when my mother phoned to tell me my father was in hospital. My small voice said: *Get on a plane NOW and go back to Scotland.* I decided my small voice was making a fuss, and planned to go in a day or two. My father died that night, and I never got to say goodbye or tell him how much I loved him.

Some years later, sitting in the kitchen with friends and my children, my small voice got me up on my feet and running through to the living room. My youngest child – a toddler – had pulled a big mirror off the wall and was lying on his back, winded, with a huge jagged piece of broken glass across his throat. I lifted the piece of glass off him and caught him up in my arms. It was a long time before I stopped shaking. My small voice hadn't used words this time, just sheer urgency.

Any time I have ignored my small voice, I have regretted it deeply. It is wiser than I am. It puts tiny invisible bits of information together and makes something true; it knows things that are below the level of consciousness. It truly is my intelligent unconscious.

I wish it would shout, would take me by the shoulders and shake me. But it doesn't work that way. Instead I have to learn to be still and listen...

An invitation: Your small voice

When have you heard your small voice?

How did you react? What did you do?

CHAPTER SEVEN

Living on the land

It is indeed hard work, living in the open in a tent. The sand and dust are everywhere. My hair is matted with dust and flattened by my sun hat during the day, my woolly hat by night. Brushing it vigorously makes me feel better, but I have no mirror, and, after a day or so, no vanity.

It takes quite a few of those qualities I celebrate on my altar, notably resilience and persistence, to live out in the open – above all a sense of humour, and a keen eye for the ridiculous.

Getting to my quest site was pure farce. We had been told to bring only what we could carry, so I had reduced everything to one bag; but with tent, sleeping bag, sleeping mat, tarpaulin and a few spare clothes, its weight was at the limit of what I could manage. On the first day I got it down myself to our communal campsite but getting it from there to my quest site was trickier, as somehow, although I had added nothing extra, things just wouldn't go neatly back into the bag again. So my guide got me a wheelbarrow. We set off, my guide leading, me pushing my laden wheelbarrow, and three of the helpers bringing up the rear. I manoeuvred the wheelbarrow over the rough ground, avoiding as much as possible the delicate plants and fungi. It stuck in the sand, went off at an angle, almost tipped, and the helpers offered to help; it was, after all, what they were there for. I refused. Someone suggested I turn it round and pull it, which made things a little easier. More offers of help. More refusals. This was my thing to do.

104

Then I had one of those out-of-body moments when I caught sight of myself trudging across the land with my hat crammed onto my head, tracksuit bottoms under my long skirt, looking like something from a Breughel painting of peasants in the Middle Ages. But I persevered, getting to where I was to stay, and unloading my bits from the barrow. Finally, all that was left in it was the large and heavy bag. Still I refused help, until one of the women said, 'Let me help you – for me,' and I saw how ridiculous – and selfish – I was being. It was a precious moment; it punctured my over-seriousness, it made me smile and laugh ruefully at myself. It resonated through the days of my quest, and beyond. Any time now that I find myself pushing relentlessly forward, I stop and laugh, and acknowledge a wheelbarrow moment.

This happens when sewing the wilding map – in my journal, I write:

Sewing the green thread – done (initially) in the spirit of wheelbarrow. Got more and more complicated and wrong. Increasingly resentful – then POW! Bring in grace – simplify – now better, clearer, faster, cleaner and POW! How to make it FUN next time – beads and ribbons and joy!

I find that moments of shifting often happen when I laugh at myself. Some years ago, I was bemoaning my domestic situation to a woman friend: 'I'm just a doormat,' I said. 'No you're not,' my friend replied. 'You're a fitted carpet.' We laughed until we cried, and something inside me shifted.

An invitation: Laughter

When was the last time you laughed at yourself? With
compassion, with empathy, with love?

Back on the land

Daily life here on my quest is simple. It gives me time to figure out how I can make wilding a way of living, a daily practice. The Buddhists say: 'Before enlightenment, hew wood and draw water. After enlightenment, hew wood and draw water.' My enlightenment, my moment of insight about my wilding self, isn't anything unless I know how to live it day by day, moment by moment. It takes practice, and I have to feel my way into the practice.

How do I use this quest time to explore what wilding is for me? How do I continue to learn and use and be my wilding? I have a few precious days here in the high desert and must use them well and wisely.

There are a lot of parallels between spiritual life and the practicalities of the physical: they are both uncomfortable and need hard work. Hew wood and draw water...

The days develop their own rhythm, emerging from the work I am doing, from my physical need for food and rest, from the heat of the sun and the sharp cold of the night, from my guide's visits and the food and water brought every evening. Food eaten outdoors, eaten in the company of birds, relished with hunger, is very special. Tastes become vivid and textures intriguing.

I have to take medication three times a day: at seven in the morning, at midday and at five in the afternoon. Although there are no electronic devices allowed, no books, or text of any kind, I have permission for a small battery-powered alarm clock to keep track of the strict regime. But I realise that sunrise is seven o'clock in the morning and, waking in the predawn light, I can take my pills as the sun comes above the mountain range opposite. Midday is simple to work out with the sun overhead, so in a moment of inspiration, I make a sundial. There is a small tree stump with a twig sticking out of the top just beyond my altar. When the shadow from the twig reaches the centre of a white stone (I move it just a bit for symmetry) it is midday. And when the shadow stretches out long across the earth to line up with a small plant (I add another stick to make sure that I don't inadvertently stand on it) then it is time for my five o'clock pills. It is so good to put the clock away.

As it moves through the day, the shadow's path describes a long shallow curve, one half of an oval: very beautiful and elegant. Somehow, I had imagined – if I had ever thought about it at all – that the shadow would travel in a straight line. I wonder about the mathematics that govern such an extraordinary arabesque. Back home, writing this, I look up the mathematics of sundials and there it is, a simple elegant oval.

It is deeply satisfying living by the sun and the moon, stepping free of the clock and its tyranny. I go to bed at nightfall, when the light fades, and rise at dawn when the light rises. Time is no longer linear, but all-encompassing. I have moved from Chronos time, with its seconds and hours measured and prescribed, to Kairos time, fully present in each moment and simultaneously infinite. Many years ago, I heard Dr Leroy LittleBear of the Blackfoot tribe talking about how his language has words for today, yesterday, the day before yesterday, tomorrow, the day after tomorrow, and a long time. He paused, looked about the lecture theatre filled with academics, and added 'in any direction'. There was a collective intake of breath, and I swear I heard a hundred and fifty brains imploding.

I am also acutely aware of the privilege of these days, of my guide and her helpers' loving holding, of the time out of time that I have been able to gift myself. This is time for me, for contemplation, for learning and discovering what I think, who I am, where I want to change and grow. After a lifetime of tending other people's gardens – to continue the metaphor – here I am tended to, nourished physically and mentally, emotionally and spiritually.

It is opening up the time and space to do the deep dive into myself that is happening with creating the map.

As I said, being on the land like this for this length of time is very challenging – not just the night-time waking, and the daytime heat, not just the dust and the sand, or the lumpy bumpy ground I am sleeping on, which slopes gently downhill leaving me bundled against the door of my tent and having to wriggle back up each time I wake, but the emotional work I am doing during the day and processing overnight.

Halfway through my quest, I wake sobbing uncontrollably in the middle of the night, not knowing why, in exhaustion and despair. And then something shifts – I find that there is no separation between me and the earth. The lumps and bumps of the ground, the inexorable slide downhill are gone, and I am held in warmth and comfort and love. It is an extraordinary feeling. There is no separation between me and Mother Earth – I lie on her breast as my own new-born children lay on mine.

I sleep.

When I wake, just before sunrise, and deeply refreshed, I tell Pedernal what happened. 'Look behind you,' she says, and as I turn, I realise I have been cradled between her and Grandmother Tree. These two strong eternal women – the mountain and the tree – have held me gently and firmly when I most needed it. I finally understand that Mother Earth is just that, my mother. Not an abstract concept, but a living, breathing, conscious entity that wants so deeply – that yearns – to live in harmony, peace and balance with all the different parts of herself, all her children. The love and warmth that I felt from the earth as I lay there – the sheer relief, the security, the calm – is with me even now. As a small child, if I couldn't sleep, my mother would snuggle me into bed by folding the pillow up around my ears and tucking the bedding under it to hold in position. I felt safe and held and would fall asleep easily and deeply. This feels the same.

And I start to understand how the earth feels. After the births of my three children, they were put gently on my breast as I lay exhausted; euphoric at the end of the labour, at the fact of a healthy child, at the overflow of love I felt for each of them, amazement and gratitude to my body, to those who had helped me – husband, midwives and carers. The body of each child – though so very different from one another – fitted perfectly onto the curves and angles of mine, skin to skin, breath to breath rising and falling, hearts beating in sympathy. The physicality of the moment, the visceral quality of my love for my child, is what I feel from the earth. Truly, Mother Earth holding me, new-born on her breast, Grandmother Tree helping.

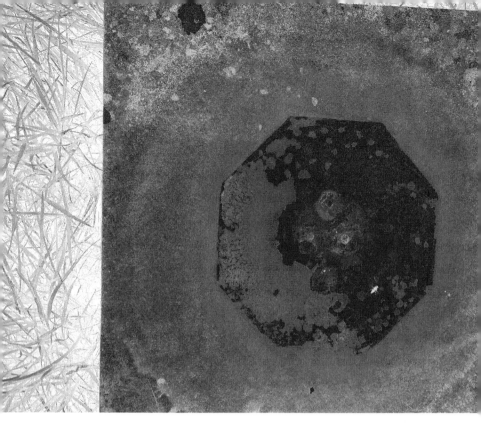

Wild Birth

STORY 12

I left the building and walked quickly away down the grassy slope, gulping fresh lungfuls of crisp Scottish air, and went down through the grounds to a more level area, shielded by the hill from the house above, and from the road out - the wider world - by a line of trees. I sank gratefully to my knees on the cool earth, the soft grass. My friend had accompanied me, no doubt concerned by my urgent 'I've just got to get out' from inside the training programme we were part of, and also wise enough to know that something important was going on. She sat quietly by, unobtrusively supportive and expectant, like a midwife.

I was torn between my natural rationality and self-consciousness (*What am I doing here? What must this look like?*) and the urgent commands from my body. I was on my knees in the grass, but not still, my body constantly moving, from some rhythm within. I reached my hands down to the grass. I had to be on all fours.

My body was moving involuntarily. Something was moving my body. I flexed up and back, arching, my pelvis rocking. *Am I actually possessed?* I wondered; caught up in some collective fantasy from the deep practitioner work we had been training in? My pelvis rocked, I rocked forward and back on all fours. Recognition; something of this was stored already in my muscle memory. 'This is how I gave birth,' I said.

And as I allowed myself on those two occasions before when I gave birth to my children, I let my body take the lead. 'It knows what it's doing, let it happen,' I soothed myself internally, still a part of me hoping no one could see my weird gyrations in the grass.

The currents in my body grew stronger and I let the tide take me. Somewhere deep in the womb of me, something was being generated, my hips constantly rocking back and forward, back and forward.

It felt like sex and I had a sudden gnosis that the opening to birth, the deep opening to life to bring life, was preceded by a similar opening where the masculine and feminine energies met and created. And in this moment now, I could feel the forces of the feminine and the masculine moving in me. Birth was not a purely feminine act. And then it was as if I could sense and experience the pure forces of creation around me, almost see them working, felt the raw unstoppable power of the feminine and masculine coming together to create life. It was every blade of grass, every breath of wind in every leaf on every tree, every cell in my pulsating body, and the energy of worlds moving in my womb connecting to every particle of life rose, rose, rose and my openness, my opening wide to the earth stretched, opened me further, beyond all experience, still the feminine and masculine forces dancing together in perfect union, until the intensity softened and my awareness of the connection of all life was something known rather than held. Resonating still but not all-consuming. Part of my consciousness returned to the real world around me as the rocking in my pelvis subsided. Self-consciousness returned, as I again wondered if anyone had seen this – whatever this was.

My patient friend by my side the whole time, like a midwife, checking in on me. My body still moving gently, the rhythm fading, everything still in my cells, like a dream fading into a deeper place than memory.

'You just gave birth,' my patient midwife said.

And I knew I had birthed myself. My full, true, raw, animal, divine, connected, powerful woman-self. That powerful woman-me, that had been denied me for so long, locked away from me, was birthed through me, through my small, contracted self. And She whom I had carried all along, sleeping in my bones, was born. And took her right place in the world.

CHAPTER EIGHT

Walking the wilding path

*The question is always - how will I live in a
wilding way in my day-to-day life, with all its
joys and indignities, its commonplace routines?
How will I sustain the insights, the ways of
being, loving and doing once I return home?*

A safe space

The quest is a safe space for me to practice living in a wilding way: if I can
discover it here, practice it here, then I can take it back with me into my
daily life. If in this bounded space, confronting myself in all my different
facets, I can glimpse what it means to live in a wilding way on the wilding
path, then I have the chance of taking that back home into the world of
people, roadworks, and phones. And hot showers.

Talking with my guide about the wilding path, we explore it as a daily
meditation. How do I find and walk the wilding path day by day, moment
by moment, in a practical way? I answer my own question: any time I don't
know what to do, I can ask: What does my wilding say? I write in my journal:

*Trusting that my wilding will know how to react, what to say, in any situation. So I
don't have to rehearse. And that if my wilding doesn't know, then I will say so, and
that I have to think about it.*

As well as creating the wilding map, I have other tasks during my week's
quest, tasks that explore alternative ways of approaching these day-to-day

dilemmas, ways of being in the world. I see them as gifts, gifts of resilience and thoughtfulness that I can practice while I am on my quest and take home to sustain me on my wilding path.

But before I can fully walk the wilding path, I need to clear it. What is blocking my path?

Clearing the pathways

What has stopped you? my guide asks. What are the old hold-backs?

In the wilding metaphor, what has been blocking the light? Pot-binding my roots? Drying out and starving the soil? Cutting down the hedgerows, ploughing up the meadows and the wildflowers? Poisoning the insects and the birds?

My task is to identify these old hold-backs – the stuck attitudes and habits of behaviour, the stinking thinking – and ask what is their new energy, their new work. They have kept me safe in the past, and for that I must thank them and appreciate their work. Now it is time for them – for me – to let go of that old purpose and start their new work.

What has held me back? In my journal:

Appeasement, guilt, embarrassment, being nice (in order to be liked), low self-esteem, ducking it and procrastination, fear of missing out, dissociation.

I go through the list, thinking back to all the times I have used these blocks to hide behind: appeasement kept me safe when I was living in volatile situations, but often at the expense of fudging the truth.

Guilt was so heavy when I picked up responsibility for other people's behaviour as well as my own.

Embarrassment blocked me from being open and truthful to others and to myself.

Being nice in order to be liked so often meant disguising what I really felt or thought.

My low self-esteem prevented me from accepting compliments or believing people when they said how good my work was.

Procrastination and ducking things deflected my capacity to move with clarity and power.

Fear of missing out made me jump in and offer to do things when I really had no time or space to do them properly, and so letting other people – and myself – down badly.

And finally, dissociation meant I buried my true feelings deep inside me when things were bad, rather than tackling the issues head-on and honestly.

It's interesting – and heartening – how many of these I've been working on with some success. It's fascinating – and no longer disheartening – how many of these are still alive and kicking. Or were, until at the start of my quest, I looked back up the path and said goodbye to my life up until this time, and goodbye to these barriers as well.

And I know at the same time that these hold-backs are the tip of an old and deep iceberg.

How to do it

I work my way through the list I have made and give thanks to each hold-back in turn for their historical role in keeping me safe. There are eight in all. Then I ask them each to find their new role with me moving forward, in growing my wilding self.

The energy of appeasement with its illusion of safe-keeping and its distortion of reality, into what might just (but never did) stave off danger can now be used to see that reality clearly, to speak that truth openly. Mark Twain said, 'I always tell the truth. That way I don't have to remember anything.'

There was a time in my life when I was fearful of telling the truth because of what I thought might happen if I did. So I fudged the truth, or lied, to whoever it was I felt I needed to appease. Sometimes this was about simple things – I remember fudging the truth to my (now ex-) husband about the time I had agreed to collect my son from the babysitter: 'It's okay, they're flexible, there's no rush.' But they weren't flexible, they were very cross and never babysat for me again. And I was left with trying, unsuccessfully, to appease them.

I realise now that it is a long time since I have done this, and it is such a relief to feel and acknowledge the peace that comes from being free of those labyrinthine evasions. I write *Your energy can gloriously bring me into balance and serenity.*

So the energy of appeasement becomes the wilding energy of Speak-my-truth, Guardian of balance and serenity.

Getting in touch

There are so many moments in my life where I have experienced a pivot. I am in one now, and yet this is not the one I will speak about here. I am going to take you back in time to my late teens.

To this point in my short life, I feel as though I have spent it conforming. To the whims and wishes of my mother and stepfather, to society, to the archetype of 'being a teenage girl/woman', to my friends in an attempt to keep up with them, to my teachers, to my school (the list literally could go on and on) so in summary, to everything in fact.

And in that conforming I am uncomfortable. I literally am not comfortable in my own skin. I am not myself; I am figuratively others' versions of me – what I think I should be in order to fit in. A stranger looks back at me from the looking glass. Certainly, inside I feel less than 'normal', falling short when I compare myself to the world. This is of course in lots of ways – I see and behave differently to others; life feels somehow more complex for me. Especially though, as I write this, I am thinking about in the world of intimate love, where the talk and expectation is of boyfriends and marriage and babies... and... that just does not feel like the right path for me. I met a man – the kindest most gentle and creative man – handsome too – and really,

deep down, what I wanted was his friendship... unsurprisingly, we drifted about, and then, apart.

And then I meet a woman and a whirlwind of confusion enters my head and heart. We meet socially and flirt and giggle and connect deeply in fun. I have actual butterflies floating about in my tummy. We meet again, and again, and after months of this we kiss and I stay the night, and my world turns upside down. The next morning – terror, joy, fear, happiness – a see-saw of emotions as I drive home to shower and change and get to work. How will I tell my friends, my family, myself? Because... finally everything makes sense. I make sense! This is what has been missing for me – an understanding of my sexuality. Literally, my whole life is suddenly clear, my image of self razor sharp.

A year of heartache (as I came out to family and friends) and wonderment followed. And ultimately, heartbreak. She was stronger than me.

This was and is my wilding path: to see and be me, no matter what others think – a proud, gay woman... (amongst other things!).

The energy of guilt is something I find I have already dealt with, and now is the time to celebrate my freedom from it. I used to walk around with an imaginary rucksack on my back, filling it with rocks of guilt I picked up as I went through life. Guilt for things I had or hadn't done; guilt for other people's behaviours that I felt responsible for – how often had I found myself apologising for someone else's actions, actions over which I had no control and for which I had no responsibility. The imaginary rucksack filled with imaginary guilt-rocks weighed me down so much I sometimes felt immobilised by the sheer bulk of it.

Now I ask: 'Is this mine to deal with?' and if it isn't, I put it down and walk away. And if it is mine to deal with, then I make amends, I apologise, and – most importantly of all – I figure out how not to repeat the behaviour that has caused the guilt in the first place. I have taken out the guilt-rocks that don't belong to me and walked easier for it; I have made amends for things I have done/not done, said/not said and gradually emptied the rucksack. And now I deal with any wrong I do as soon as I realise it. Keep the rucksack empty.

The energy of guilt becomes the wilding energy of Own-my-own, Guardian of discernment.

The energy of embarrassment is so close to the energy of guilt. In my journal I write:

> Nine times out of ten the embarrassment will be in my own head, but for that tenth time it is worth taking the risk, catching myself at it, and laughing at the absurdity of it all.

Embarrassment can also tip into shame, and if it does it becomes very toxic. We are only as sick as our secrets. Writing our wilding story can help clear the secrets by exposing them to the fresh air. And so often the secret turns out to be absurd, and I can laugh it away.

The energy of embarrassment becomes the wilding energy of Laughter, Guardian of absurdity.

The energy of being nice, wanting to be liked, is a longstanding condition that still lingers. As Alice Munro says, 'There is no seduction like that of being thought a good girl'.

I was brought up with the idea that there is a 'right' way to be a woman. Good women are modest, charming, polite and unobtrusive, content to earn – on average in the UK, 16.4% – less than their male counterparts, and to pick up the double load of career and caring for the children, the house, elderly parents. 'Good' women are liked. 'Bad' women are those who don't play that game; 'bad' women are disliked.

Reluctance to speak out, to 'make a fuss', to go against what is expected – however harmful (and it sometimes/often is), takes courage, takes practice, and above all takes conviction – that I am a person with ideas, with thoughts worth paying attention to, with needs and personal and societal boundaries. That I am, in fact, a remarkable woman. And paradoxically, niceness, I write in my journal, *is more likely to repel people than attract them.*

The energy of being nice hides layers of fear and anxiety, so I call on this energy to transform itself into the energy of true warmth from the heart, from the soul: the energy of abundance.

The energy of being nice to be liked becomes the wilding energy of Soul-warmth, Guardian of abundance.

The energy of low self-esteem, of 'impostor syndrome', has blocked me for many years in my artwork, my writing, my professional and academic life. When I completed my time as an art student, I was offered the chance of a place at the Royal College of Art and turned it down so I could do secretarial training to fit in with my then husband's plans. I contrast this with how it felt when I finished my Viva (the oral defence of my PhD thesis): at that moment I knew more about my subject than anyone else in the world, and I knew that I knew that. Now I can tap into that quiet confidence whenever I feel off-balance or diminished.

When I spoke to the energy of low self-esteem, it spoke straight back to me: 'Stand in your own power!'

So the energy of low self-esteem becomes the wilding energy of Stand-in-my-power, Guardian of grace.

And the important thing is...

And so, to now. A pandemic that felt far removed from me in the first weeks of reporting as I lived my incredibly rushed life. Travel, work, planes, trains, work, more work, juggling, no space for anything else... busy, busy, busy... no matter, I am fit and strong and healthy!

Then, a dry cough and the loss of taste and smell – and still I worked, not really paying attention – almost making light of the fact that I might have 'IT'. A week later I was floored. Many trips and a couple of stays in hospital and a more than six-month recovery journey as Covid wreaked havoc on my vascular system... I was forced to stop. The universe sent me a message: '...take stock – your time is limited and how you are choosing to live is not suiting you, or me...' it said.

I listened. I feel as though I have been given the gift of life. I feel lucky, loved and blessed to have had the chance to think again.

My pivot then – to only work on projects and with people that give me energy. To work on things that will truly make a difference – either to humanity or the planet – and to be clear on how much time I will give that. To allow space for love, happiness and creativity. To be at home more, to invest time with friends and family to be more present in the here and now. To worry less about money and to hold the faith that when I let go, I will let come.

In doing this I will allow myself time to enjoy nature and my new-found yoga practice and to have fun, laughter, silliness and abundance in my life – as well as to know I am making an impact that matters to the world.

This, all of this, brings me pleasure and happiness... it's funny how a near-death experience can sharpen one's wits!

I asked ducking it and procrastination to transform its considerable energy, energy which has over the years added so much extra guilt about things not done, into 'doing it' energy; to move, as I wrote, *From ducking it to doing it. And to do what is mine to do, not anyone else's.* This book is one glorious result.

So the energy of ducking it becomes the wilding energy of Quiet action, Guardian of timeliness and peace.

The fear of missing out (FOMO) has ruled my life for years, the urge to be helpful, to be invasively proactive, to jump in at the deep end where angels fear to tread – to mix a number of metaphors. The feeling that everything worth doing was round the next corner, and the next, and the next, just glimpsed and always elusive. Again, I write: *Is it mine to do?* There is a quiet joy in waiting for the moment of inspiration, and a wild ecstatic joy in moving when inspiration, not just anything, happens.

So the energy of fear of missing out becomes the wilding energy of Inspiration, Guardian of Inspiration.

The repetition soothes and comforts me. This Guardian is placed with Pedernal, an inspiring and quiet presence.

The energy of dissociation had sent me deep inside myself when things were bad, burying my feelings so far down that I lost all sense of what was real, and what was happening. I realise that – mostly – I am living in a real present, and – mostly – tackling issues head-on and honestly when they arise.

I call on the energy of dissociation to transform into the wilding energy of Powerful presence, Guardian of connection.

Christmas Day

Think of ordinary situations: entering or leaving a room, putting down a book, using a hand towel, making a passing remark. When my father was in the house, these and countless other trivial actions carried with them a sense of suspense and dread.

Had you caused a disturbance, been overly casual, replaced the towel in the wrong way, said something out of place? He had the ability to insert dread into daily activities without the need to say anything. If we were laughing and he came in, we would fall silent. Silliness, spontaneity, frivolity were among the many things that were frowned upon. No view that ran contrary to his own could be tolerated. Sentences needed to be perfectly formed and carefully thought out. We were permanently on tenterhooks. My mother might place his supper in front of him only to have it pushed away in disgust. The plates would be too cold, too hot, the food too much, too little, too cooked, not cooked enough, too repetitive, the wrong colour, not the right consistency. Although the act of disapproval was churlish, the mood was much darker, and no one contradicted him. Fear stopped us, but not the fear of a raised voice or hand. The fear was of being stifled yet further by the tension that already hung heavy in the room.

My mother, a fiercely intelligent, well-read and educated woman, dealt with his demands and criticisms without complaint. When it came to mealtimes, she took the food back, reheated it, left it to cool, gave him more, re-cooked it and tried every other possible means to avoid unpleasantness. Again, never a raised voice. Never an expression of her own frustration or disappointment. Never, most of all, any indication that his demands were unreasonable. She was clearly the one at fault; he had a right to expect better.

That changed during a Christmas lunch in 1995, a full three and half decades into her marriage. It was early afternoon and already the darkness was gathering in the room. One of my father's many oddities was a dislike of lighting, so the room remained in shadow. As usual, the atmosphere was tense and he was finding fault, sharply and cruelly, with something she had done and as she moved to remedy whatever it was that was annoying him, she glanced at me. Nothing could have been more unlike her. It was a half-smile, a fleeting, almost imperceptible moment in which she caught my eye and in doing so she expressed a rebellion that shattered the outward veneer of passive acceptance. That's all it was. Nothing changed. He died after sixty years of marriage having never even boiled a kettle, but from that moment I knew where she stood and who she backed.

There are more hold-backs, the more I think about it. Hypervigilance, for example. There have been times in my life when I have lived under coercive control. Hypervigilance helped keep me safe, to tell by the sound of a footstep or the closing of a door just what might be coming next, and to get out of the way or prepare myself for it. But hypervigilance has become a block, where I over-interpret what I am perceiving. I mistake simple things for sinister intent and start to project into a future that may never happen.

Now I can thank it for keeping me safe in difficult times and appreciate its emerging new role – a hyper-awareness of the beauty of the world around me. As my lovely friend WindSong says: 'If you're not in awe, you're not paying attention.' Hypervigilance now connects me to the natural world, to the extraordinary nature of the ordinary, noticing how the dust motes play in the air, or the shadows dapple my path as I walk through the trees on my way to my studio, or the texture of the ground beneath my shoes, or the taste of a single honeysuckle flower plucked on my way past a bush.

In my closing ceremony on the last night of my quest, I speak the name and the new power of each Guardian, and give each one a place on the land, anchoring them in my memory. Speak-my-truth is in the tree that guards the entrance to my quest site, my wilding place. Own-my-own is in the juniper tree opposite. Soul-warmth is with Grandmother Tree. The others are with the roots of trees, with my altar, with the sundial, and with Pederal herself. The final Guardian, Powerful-Presence: Guardian of Connection, is held in the whole wilding place.

These Guardians are special gifts of my quest, the shift in my spirit and my soul that I can call on when my wilding self is faltering. They set out principles of living that transcend the pull of personalities. They are strong, powerful women that stand forward to hold me in my power and strength: balance and serenity, discernment, absurdity, timeliness and peace, abundance, grace, inspiration, connection.

As I meet them each morning, and thank them each night, their power grows in me.

An invitation: Clearing the pathways

What are your hold-backs? What blocks your path to wilding?
What do you need to deal with? Go back to the start of this
section and follow the process that I did.

This is important work – give yourself as much space and time as
you need, with uninterrupted quiet and peace.

Use coloured pens or felt-tips, and a large plain notebook or
sketchpad. Leave plenty of space in the notebook – you will most
likely want to return to your Guardians as you grow into them,
to add new insights to what is already there; perhaps to add a
completely new Guardian.

Messages from the land

At the start of this story I talked about my day of preparation for the quest. I described my time by the sea, listening for what Mother Earth would tell me, and how her messages formed the basis of the letter of intention I had sent.

On our first day on the land, before we set off for our quest sites, each seeker went out alone to prepare for their quest.

I walked onto the land, waiting and looking for whatever would come. What came was powerful:

My eye was caught by a flight of pinyon jays from the east, so I followed them. They led me to a tree – a pinyon pine – and I sat quietly under its branches, watching and listening, becoming aware of the wind's cold touch on my skin, of the sun's heat. The landscape seemed to breathe; each breath releasing a butterfly, a cicada, a bird, a cottonwood leaf blown up from the bottom of the canyon; each breath intensifying the colours of the cacti – tall yellow flowers and squat black nodules – the silver greys of the shadows, the luminous blue of the New Mexico sky. The light itself seemed to breathe. And I sat, transfixed by the landscape's intensity: its colour, its sounds, its shapes, its movements, all playing out in front of me.

Out of this the message came: Be intensely and simply in the moment.

I sat quiet and still for some time, breathing with the landscape, just being.

Then I waited, trusting I'd get a sign for my next message, and a chipmunk scurried across the landscape. I'd only ever seen chipmunks on film, and even then they had mainly been animated talking animals, so I hadn't realised just how small they are – smaller than our Scottish red squirrels, and much faster. So I followed it, as it dashed in two bursts – a zig and a zag – towards a shaded rock – perfect to be out of the sun.

But there were ants feasting on a crushed juniper berry just where I wanted to sit, so I went round the other side. There was a hole – a kind of cavern –

beneath the rock, and I felt uneasy about it. Our guide had said that the snake people were going to sleep, and that if we disturbed any of them, we should simply and quietly move away from them with apologies for disturbing their peace. I decided that this was a bit further than I wanted to go right now on my first full medicine day, even though I'm certain I'd have come to no harm, so I moved into the sun on top of some nearby rocks.

I could hear the cicadas, loud in the middle of the day. Although I had a hat, and my arms and legs were well covered against the sun, I felt it burning on the backs of my hands and realised that I hadn't brought any salve with me. I had to be my own salve. So I moved into the shade cast by some ancient juniper trees. Their twisted trunks and branches were patterned like flowing water, like the passage of the streams – the burns – that cascade down the side of Scottish mountains, weaving in and out of the rocks and the tiny islands of heather clumps, cool, noisy, light where the sun catches them, dark in the sudden deeps where they disappear below ground. Like the boulders at the top of the canyon that held the marks of being worn smooth by water millennia ago, so these ancient trees seem to hold a visual memory in their bark of water deep underground. Cool, and cooling my hands.

The ground was scattered with discarded cicada shells, old exoskeletons, the shells of the cicada pupae as they emerge into adulthood. In Greek and Roman myth, the cicada signifies carefree living and immortality. I wondered at the metaphor – to live carefree it was necessary to shed my shell and to emerge into adulthood. I had always thought of carefree-ness (is there such a word?) as being the prerogative of childhood, when the child doesn't have to worry about food and shelter and safety – or at least not in some parts of the world.

From where I sat, I could see Pedernal and her generous grasp and reach, the sloping shoulders on either side of the central flat-topped peak like arms reaching out and holding me. Salve and shade.

The message came: Casting off my shell, my exoskeleton; salve and shade my means.

I ate my lunch. And mused on this message. Carefree living, joyful living, possible through being, becoming, fully adult. Adult in the sense of being responsible for myself, caring for myself, finding shade or remembering salve, remembering the flow of water hidden in plain sight in the trees' bark, hearing the cicada singing, leaving the ants and the snake people in peace to enjoy their crushed berries, their cool burrows. The thought of living a carefree adult life is one I continue to mull over.

It was time to listen for another message.

There was a vista, a long view, through the trees shading me. Although it looked like a path, there was no track, but I felt strongly this was the way I should be going, so I clambered over rough ground, stooped under branches, skirted the delicate ground fungi and the needle-sharp cacti. A yellow butterfly led me to where I was supposed to be, hovering until I caught up with it, waiting patiently as I detoured round obstacles, moving back and forth over the path that wasn't a path, until we reached the right place, under the partial shade of another juniper tree. A small brown butterfly, just glimpsed, said 'yes' to it.

There was a tall cactus with two yellow flowers, thick-petalled and almost tree-ringed. I decided to sit quietly with closed eyes and see what emerged. As I looked down, I noticed my fingernails were dirty, so I cleaned them with a twig – and a raven croaked at me to get me back on track. Then my nose needed blowing, and if it wasn't my body fidgeting, it was my mind. Then I started to check the time (this was before all clocks and watches were left behind) – three o'clock in the afternoon.

I closed my eyes again for a few minutes, perhaps five, and dozed off with dreams, and swaying with my Parkinson's dyskinesia, the curious weaving movement that is a side-effect of the dopamine drugs.

The message came: Stillness – getting beyond fidgeting and distraction. Accept my body as it is right now.

This time there was no ambiguity, no mistaking the message, even with the raven telling me off. There was no one there to distract me, no one I could blame my inattention on; the stillness had to come from inside me.

Now for the fourth and final message.

I followed the path leading up to the main building on the quest land. As I did, the wind increased. Another darting chipmunk caught my eye, and my curiosity, and led me to a series of tiny bright-yellow flowers. I played stepping stones to avoid the black ground fungi and ended up sitting in front of a magnificent circular clump of very spiny cacti. Pedernal was behind a tree to my right and the sun was on my back.

I slept a little and rested. The sun was lowering, slowly, almost imperceptibly. My shadow was very clear – hat tilting, shoulder lifted. The wind softened, warm and gentle, it didn't have to be fierce and blow your hat off. As I wrote this it strengthened again – was it blowing clarity into my heart-mind? Beyond softness? Fierce and gentle by turns.

Curiosity. Einstein said: 'I have no special talent, I am only passionately curious.' Does softness equal lack of clarity? Is clarity dependent on fierceness? Does softness equal lack of clarity, but gentleness is a different kind of clarity?

The message came: Clarity through curiosity; clarity through fierceness; clarity through gentleness.

I wrote each message on a long strip of canvas and hung them from one of Grandmother Tree's branches. As I grew deeper day by day into the quiet of the land and the energy of the map I was creating, the messages resonated every time I needed them.

I was getting muddled? The fourth message reminded me of clarity through curiosity, fierceness and gentleness.

Distracted? The third message brought me back to accepting my body and to stillness.

Dwelling on the past? The first message led my eyes to the intensity of the fierce blue sky, and my heart-mind to being simply and intensely present, in the present.

Feeling isolated or alone? The second message challenged me to discard my shell and connect with my deeper self and reminded me that I could do it, knew how to do it, and had the means.

When I woke – as I always did – in the middle of the night, it was often with a question on my mind. I'd mull over the messages the four directions had sent me, and inevitably there would be one I couldn't remember; and that was always the one I needed. The night before I started work on the map, I woke remembering a pupil of mine – an amateur painter who had a strong innate talent. He was a competent, if naïve, artist who one day got to the edge of something bigger and greater – then stepped back. We were working on new ways of looking and seeing, turning the landscape into simple blocks of shape and colour, semi-abstract, in a way that bypassed the judgemental part of the brain and opened infinite possibilities of image. He knew he could do it – in fact, he started to make intense and lovely marks on the paper – then he stopped. 'No,' he said, 'I won't do it. I'm happy as I am.' And went back to his naïve detailed filled-in watercolour sketches.

In my journal I wrote:

> Remembering how G pulled back from making the leap forward into another level of painting/seeing and stayed with what he was comfortable with.
>
> Am I at the same threshold spiritually?

The messages from the four directions tell me, clearly and simply, that yes, I am at the same spiritual threshold, and no, I will not pull back from it.

Be intensely and simply in the moment.

Casting off my shell, my exoskeleton; salve and shade my means.

Stillness – getting beyond fidgeting and distraction. Accept my body as it is right now.

Clarity through curiosity; clarity through fierceness; clarity through gentleness.

Each day I stitch my meditation, and paint, and write. This practice comes back with me when I return home to Scotland. Each day I reflect on my learning, on what I have done to walk with the wilding.

An invitation: Asking the earth

Mother Earth holds a deep wisdom that we can access through honing our awareness and stillness. Do you have a decision to make? A choice to accomplish?

Frame it as a question and take it to Mother Earth. Hold the question lightly in your mind and walk in nature. What do you notice? Hear? Smell? Feel? Sense?

Maybe an answer is emerging...

Body awareness

My body gives me messages and learning I need and am often too thrawn (a good Scots word meaning stubborn, single-minded, and even pig-headed) to listen to.

When I left Scotland to fly to New Mexico I had a slight cold. After spending three very special days with my Medicine Sister, WindSong, in Connecticut, my cold had shifted from 'slight' to 'heavy'. By the time I arrived at the land, I had almost completely lost my voice. I could croak in an exaggerated stage whisper, but that was all.

'What's this all about?' I asked my guide sotto voce.

'You'll just have to listen,' she said.

Did you know that the letters of LISTEN also spell SILENT? Did you know that we can't listen unless we are silent? That we can't truly hear what is being said if we are working out in our own minds how we are going to reply, or add to, what is being said.

So in the first day with my fellow seekers, losing my voice means I have to choose my few words carefully. The pace of my thoughts is also slowed, because all my fellow seekers are Japanese. The shift from Japanese to English and back again, skilfully done by two translators, means my thoughts can no longer race ahead. I have to stay in the moment, word by word.

In his poem *Hymns to the Silence*, John Montague talks about walking in Ireland with 'Bracken and briar restraining our march/Clawing us back/ Slowing us to perception's pace...'. In the words of the poem, I have to slow my thoughts to perception's pace.

The message I was given by the west on my first day, to accept my body as it is right now, continues to resonate. I have developed a keen sense of interoception – the capacity to perceive what is happening inside one's body – which gives me the capacity to fine-tune how I keep my Parkinson's symptoms under control. Checking in with my body, I can become aware if my energy levels are flagging, or my ability to concentrate is slipping, or my head-sticking-forward posture (the despair of my personal trainer) is becoming worse, and I can do whatever I know will counter the slippage – exercise, meet up with friends, more exercise.

It has taken years to get to this point, to be aware of, and respectful of my body as more than just something to carry my head around on. To understand that I am my body, that my gut and my heart have brains as well as the goop in my skull. To understand, too, that I am completely responsible for my own wellness. No one else can exercise for me. No one else can cut down the amount of dairy and sugar that contributes to my internal inflammation and raised blood sugar levels. Only I can get myself to bed in time to have a full seven or eight hours of restorative sleep. Sara Riggare, a Swedish person with Parkinson's, counted up the number of hours she spends with her health professionals each year: 1.5 hours; and the number of hours a year she is responsible for her own wellbeing: 8,752.5 hours.

All through my quest I hold my body awareness, accepting it as it is right now, and making changes as I become aware of them. I accept and drink a special herbal tea for my cold, I sit in stillness when I am not working on the wilding map, I exercise every day on my small piece of land even if only a few Tai Chi moves. Sometimes I dance.

When we all come off the land at the end of our quests and gather in a circle to celebrate and share and honour our experiences, I say loud and clear: 'I am WalksWithTrees and I have my voice back!'

Everyone cheers.

Now

STORY 16

*How old was the little girl? I don't remember.
Six? Seven? She was fearless then and fearful
had no hold on her for a long while yet. She
was small and fully magical. This was her
favourite place... anywhere. Even though little,
she'd travelled and lived in many places and
would've looked at you with uneven eyes if
you'd said 'here' was all there was.*

She knew people meant different things when they spoke. No... not because there are different languages... although she knew that too and wanted to speak all of them. She knew places could smell different, sound different – be different. She was comfortable with different, if you'd asked her. As no one did ask her she didn't explain; except while speaking with dogs, fairies and the wind. She was light and strong with a long-armed, long-legged body, perfect for climbing pine trees and could swim like a fish.

'This is my favourite place...' she said, before holding her breath while counting on her fingers. 'I'm praticking underwater swimming...' she heaved at me before the next inhale in answer to my eyes. She lived in a house on a lake – a fresh water lake – much nicer than salt water to this little woods warrior. 'You can drink it if you're thirsty, which is conevient when you play...' she said with a solemn little bow of her head. I bowed back with the best solemn I could muster.

They'd arrived late at night, and she couldn't remember how or when she'd been put to bed, but when she woke up everything was soft. The air and her body felt disappeared in lightness as she slipped out, leaving her brothers to sleep, though they have no part in this memory. This was her favourite place... anywhere! Freedom! She went straight to the lake's edge and put her toes in the water. The temperature was as perfect as the blood running through her. The lake reached out, 'Come child', she smiled and replied, 'I'm coming, lake'. She swam, then sat in the water's shallows, putting mud and sand all over herself to see how that felt while the sunshine wrapped warm kisses around her wet skin. She filled her eyes with the lake, the pine trees, birds, bugs, fish and even the water spiders though they scared her. 'You need to keep strong eyes on them in case they sneak up on you!' she told me in an absolute fit of giggles. She told me the air was full of smells – not 'scents' as no child uses that word – of fallen pine needles, mud, water and everywhere things to play with! Abruptly she put her head upside down, '...to see what that looks like,' and started humming.

Later in life I asked her if she remembered WHEN that was. She grew still to listen with darkening eyes, gently shifted her shoulders as I heard 'it was just... now'. I am not sure she even spoke.

Sarah Matalon

CHAPTER NINE

The white deerskin

*I am to record my quest on the white deerskin.
I'm not sure when or how the word 'map'
emerged, but as I worked on it, the deerskin
became a map of wilding - a wilding map.*

Maps

I have become curious about what a map is. Cartography is the art, the
science, the study of map-making, and the word comes from the ancient
Greek 'chartes' (papyrus/sheet of paper), and 'graphein' (to write). 'Map' is
a shortened form of the medieval Latin 'mappa' (cloth or napkin) 'mundi'
(of the world), a two-dimensional representation of the world as the map-
maker knew it.

I learn that a map, in its traditional European sense, is based on
the concept that a physical reality – or an imagined reality – can be
effectively translated into two dimensions through writing and drawing
on paper, or papyrus, or parchment or cloth, and shared with others.
Map-making combines science, art and technical expertise, and the
finished map should communicate, simply and without irrelevant
characteristics, the physical or imagined reality's traits and details. A
good map should set out and arrange its elements in a way that best
conveys its message to its audience (map design). As well as physical
terrain, many early maps chart the stars; the Chinese scientist Su Song
published a star map in 1092 CE.

Spiritual maps

We are familiar with maps as a way of orienting ourselves in the world physically – maps of the London Underground, of a country, of a city or town help us to find our way from one place to the next. Medieval map-makers wanted their audience to orientate themselves not only physically but spiritually as well. In the Psalter Map (1265 CE) held in the British Library in London, the known world is drawn as a circle, with Jerusalem at its centre and the British Isles in the bottom left-hand corner. The space between the circle of the map and the edge of the page represents the spiritual realm, with Christ and two angels looking down on the earth from above.

The Australian Aboriginals use oral maps – songlines – to navigate physically across the land, and also to orientate themselves spiritually and historically. The songlines chart the genealogy of the people living on that particular piece of land, the creation of the land in the Dreamtime (the Aboriginal creation myth), and its history since then to the present moment. Songlines on the earth are often mirrored by songlines in the sky, with the stars used as a compass to navigate by, as a way of predicting tides, eclipses, and as a calendar. The stars are also used as a mnemonic, a way of remembering the earth songlines.

Maps, I am discovering, are about orientating oneself in multiple realities – physical, spiritual, historical and imagined, among many others.

My map-making reflects all of these in one degree or another as the white deerskin becomes my ground for exploring and mapping wilding. Wilding is the imagined reality, the spiritual reality, the emotional reality that the map seeks to tell, simply and effectively, to everyone who views it. However, whereas cartographers largely know the physical reality they are mapping, I know – consciously know – nothing about wilding. Making, creating the map is drawing ideas out of my unconscious, and as it grows

144

day by day, it feels increasingly as if I am simply a channel for the images emerging round the wilding idea.

I have written earlier about starting the wilding map, about knowing with absolute certainty that the three concentric circles of Being, Loving, and Doing are the first images that must go onto the deerskin. And how only after the great splashes of ink create the wilding path, running diagonally from the skin's bottom left to its top right across the three circles, only then does the drawing of Grandmother Tree grow from the centre circle.

I'm using this language carefully – I never feel that I am creating an artwork. The map dictates itself to me and I just do what it tells me. It feels as if the image of its imagined and spiritual reality already exists, and I am simply tuning into it, somehow, and making it visible. This would explain how, on the rare occasions when I have an aesthetic opinion about the map, the marks I make or the stitches I sew go wrong and have to be unpicked, repainted, made into something else. If I push it, I end up with another wheelbarrow moment, and have to stop, laugh at myself, apologise to the map, and start again. The process is full of surprises – I never know what will appear next.

Poetry of an Outsider

We landed in Prague, a city built with history and art and conflict, and as I unearthed this story, I began to morph and reflect my own complicated structure.

The pretty mother was what I had absorbed from our world, as life for a woman. I spent years thinking, observing, and testing other paths but not fully acknowledging what they were. I said yes to marriage when I was finishing graduate school. I became a mother and loved the art of creating these cherished innocents. Life was easy in my Brooklyn bubble. As we grew, I became aware of the natural world that needed to nurture us, and we moved first Upstate and then across the Delaware to a cabin with a creek. The kids were softly learning in their Steiner school outside of the pressures of life and I helped them with all of myself, buying a grain mill and learning the kitchen from scratch, and reading every foreign fairy tale out loud. But as they grew stronger, they pulled away and the space that was left felt undefined.

I started in the arts but after giving birth I studied midwifery, worked at the kids' school, and even part-time in the beautiful health food store, paths that nurtured mothering. When Jens came home one day with a job offer in Prague, I wondered where the connection might be. My Czech teachers at film school had not made an impression on me to search in their direction. But here I was at their crossroad.

It's hard to imagine a change until one experiences it. Of course, I was excited about the new and foreign, but leaving my connections indefinitely and having to define myself to those who could not identify me was shocking. It was a different kind of alone. And I made this trip in my fiftieth year as a mother to teens.

I had veered away from art for the real and practical, but now I missed my own passionate stories. Poetry was flowing from my hands, and I found myself in a supportive writing group. I learned that poetry evolves at this stage of life when we become vulnerable to wisdom and perception. As I slowly let go of the humans I had given birth to, I learned a second time how difficult it is to define who we are and what a journey is. The resistance from my family and from myself to stand for change was more painful than imagined. I felt bullied on all sides.

My first passions as a child were music and dance and in my new home I reconnected, finding myself in a Czech classical choir, performing in cathedrals all over the country. To sing in these sacred spaces had always been a dream. I also immediately found a form of dance, Gaga, that was both soulful and liberating.

As I let go of giving away my creativity and instead used it to build my own artistic vessel, a path, not straight or easy, materialised, allowing me to touch and give love, while continuing to learn and listen.

What I realise now is that as I worked on the map itself during the quest and afterwards at home in Scotland, the process was enough – the act of doing, making, creating, channelling the marks on the leather, the ink, the stitches, the drawing, the paint, the beadwork – from this process I got early glimpses of what wilding might be, and intuited the meaning of the map as it emerged with the marks I was making on the leather.

Working on the leather in the high desert, I could feel the meaning of it below the surface. It isn't until now, nearly three years later, that the meaning is becoming conscious, and as I write about it, the meaning is deepening.

The wilding map, it turns out, is scalable. It is a chart not just for me or any other woman, it is a design for a family, for a group or a community of any size. The wilding map plots what happens in different aspects of life and sets it out in the form of questions. Starting from the centre, the core of the map, I reflect on what I am discovering in the map's five parts:

Being: The wilding self – the innermost circle;

Loving: The wilding path – the second circle;

Doing: The wilding way – the third circle;

Moon shadows: The wilding community – the outer circle of shadow shapes;

Moon path: A vision for the future – the lines of ink splashes.

BEING: The wilding self

The inner ring, the shadow of the trunk, is my BEING – the innermost core of me. The questions that arise are challenging: What is at the centre of me? What is at the heart of myself as a wilding woman? What is my wilding core – how am I being principled, warm, challenging? How am I growing and developing, connecting to every other being?

Using the map for a group, for a community, what is at the community's core? Or the family's heart?

These questions and their reflections will be different whenever anyone – individual woman, community or family – engages with their Being.

Grandmother Tree's trunk and eight main branches are irregular – what does each represent for me? If I let my imagination flow across the image, if I let my mind meditate on the shapes, what are the essential messages I receive from them? What are the aspects of my wilding self that need nurturing, nourishing, expressing?

Each time I go through this the messages shift – sometimes radically, often subtly.

Grandmother Tree's branches are the plain white of the deerskin. The background of the circle of Being is the vivid yellow of the New Mexico cacti flowers, the yellow of the east, the all-potential, Grandfather Sun.

I take time to reflect on my Being.

An invitation: Notebook time

In the following pages, there are questions I ask myself. As
you read, make a note of the questions, and jot down any first
thoughts you might have about your own life. Come back to your
first thoughts later and go into them more deeply.

Reflections on My Being

As I sit with the central core of the wilding map, I remember what Pedernal, sacred mountain, told me: You are a remarkable woman, and it is time to know it. And get on with it!

What is it in the centre of me, my Being, that is remarkable?

Health

One strong branch is my health. Keeping well with my Parkinson's is at the core of my being. I know that intensive physical and cognitive exercise has reversed or plateaued my motor symptoms and keeps me cognitively and emotionally balanced. It can be hard, sometimes – especially if I have a minor infection or have been overdoing it – to keep up the exercise regime I have set out for myself, but health and Being are, for me, inseparable.

This raises the question – am I less of a person when my health is poor? The messages from the four directions come to mind, and particularly the message from the west: Stillness – getting beyond fidgeting and distraction. Acceptance of how my body is right now. I have learned throughout my Parkinson's journey to detach from the predominant medical 'restitution narrative' in which 'a person is not whole, not really able, unless one is "cured"' (Stoltzfus and Schumm) and to work from the 'quest narrative' looking at how possibility in life can be created. In her wonderful paper on how dance can help people with Parkinson's to 'feel lovely,' Sara Houston quotes Arthur Frank, an academic and also a cancer patient:

'Time spent being ill ceased to be time taken away from my life. Instead, how I lived with illness became a measure of how well I could craft a life, whether I was ill or healthy. This attitude is the basis of understanding one's story as a quest narrative. Illness remains a nightmare in many ways, but it also becomes a possibility, especially for a more intimate level of connection with others.'

Principles

The next branch of my Core Being is principles. What are the principles I live by? Live with? There were many years when I lost sight of principled living, when my decisions were based on expediency, doing whatever I thought would keep me and my children safe in a chancy and uncertain emotional environment.

This is not something I am proud of, despite knowing I did the best I was capable of at the time. That best, in hindsight, can look pretty poor, but it serves as a marker, now that I have learned, as they say, to 'look back without staring'. I refer back to the Guardians I met in my quest – the Guardians of Abundance, of Own-my-own, of Inspiration and the others – who have transformed themselves, so they no longer hold me back, but rather support me on my journey. Each Guardian holds a principle, a guidance to live by. Each principle a way towards balance.

Adventure

Then there is the branch of growth, of learning, of adventure. 'Always say yes!' takes me on voyages of discovery – like this extraordinary quest, this book, this company of wilding women. Again, I have to stay balanced, and the Guardian of Inspiration, the one that used to be FOMO (fear of missing out) has to step in from time to time with wiser council. I repeat the two key questions: 'Does it grow corn?' and if so, 'Is it mine to do?'

Attitude

The branch of attitude underpins how I encounter the challenges life throws up. For example, how I manage my Parkinson's condition – am I living by a restitution narrative? Or a quest narrative? Am I living with the learned helplessness of the medical model – 'Cure me, doctor!' – rather than the empowerment of the quest narrative, of 'crafting my life', of creating a partnership with my health professionals. Words cast spells, as I

153

am always saying. What are the words, the stories, that I tell myself about myself? As Ford said: 'Whether you think you can or think you can't, you're right'.

Unconditional love

At the heart of Grandmother Tree – her trunk rather than a branch – is unconditional love. This says easy and does hard – how do I hold unconditional love for people, situations, environments, ideas that I feel threatened by or distrust?

Some years ago I was visiting a close relative in a situation that I knew would be difficult for both of us, and held the very real potential for a permanent estrangement. *Hold onto unconditional love*, I told myself. Sure enough, halfway through the visit something was said, or not said, and I felt my righteous anger surging and could see my relative's misery and antagonism rising in response. 'Hold unconditional love. Hold unconditional love. Hold unconditional love,' I repeated to myself. Over and over again I said it in my head, and gradually it moved to my heart, and to a smile, and the moment passed and our relationship turned a corner and has never looked back.

There must be as many ways of finding and expressing unconditional love as there are situations when it is needed. This way works for me – what works for you?

And how do I find unconditional love for myself?

Creativity

The branch of creativity is at the heart of my being. It is the air I breathe, the ground I stand on, the nourishment I absorb. In this place of Being my creativity exists as a force within me. How it expresses itself – how I express it – belongs with the Loving and Doing circles. Here in my core, I simply acknowledge, love and celebrate it.

There are more branches, more reflection to do, but for the moment, simply holding an awareness of the core, the centre, of the wilding map is enough.

LOVING: The wilding path

The background of this circle is the deep red ochre of the rocks in the canyon.

Each branch in the centre, when it touches the edge of the Being core and moves into the next circle, Loving, shows different aspects of itself: its principles, its practice, its passion. This is where each branch, each part of the Core Being, becomes tangible, visible. This is where my remarkableness shows up.

Between Loving and Doing, tucked into the spaces between the branches, are drawings of Grandmother Tree's clusters of pine needles. Until now I didn't know what they signified, simply that, sitting in the shade beside Grandmother Tree, they caught my eye and had to find their place in the map. They now sit on the red ochre of the Loving circle. And I realise that there are six clusters of pine needles, and I have identified six main branches, areas, of my Being. Possibly a coincidence, possibly a loving message from Grandmother Tree – and is there any difference?

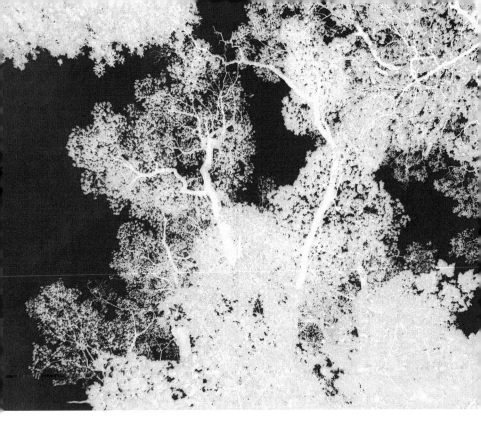

The Cardinal Bird

STORY 18

I was executive director of a non-profit contracted to provide education to individuals who had been arrested for driving while intoxicated for the first time. I hired staff who were Certified Alcohol and Drug Counselors in recovery from either alcoholism themselves (Alcoholics Anonymous) or had lived with someone who had been alcoholic (Al-Anon).

One evening I noticed one of my female counselors sitting at a desk had a very small dark red spot showing a little bit from the blouse on the left side of her chest. She was an older woman, gentle, happy but firm in her relationship to the clients we served. I said, 'Esther, do you have a tattoo?' She said, 'Yes.' She opened her blouse a bit more and showed me a very large, red cardinal bird tattoo covering the left side of her upper breast. This is her story.

She had been drinking heavily for many years and had tried to stop numerous times but always went back to drinking to the level of severe intoxication. Since she could not stop drinking, she said her self-image was at rock bottom and she no longer wanted to live. She decided to drink herself to death. She stood by her sink in the kitchen, drinking as she was looking out the window. Suddenly a bright red cardinal flew close to her window and startled her. It made her stop what she was doing, and she stopped drinking at that moment.

Several months passed and once again she was at the lowest point of her life because she couldn't stop drinking and once again decided to kill herself through alcohol and began drinking again, at the same place as before... in her kitchen, over the sink looking out her window. As she began drinking, once again a red cardinal flew close to her window, which startled her once again. This time she felt like it was more than a coincidence... she felt it was a message and decided to attend an Alcoholics Anonymous meeting. From that moment on, she never drank any alcohol.

In her recovery she decided to get a red cardinal tattoo, over her heart on her left breast. She told her husband she was going to get it and he said that if she got a tattoo he would divorce her. She said she had put him through a lot as a result of her drinking but this was important to her. She told him she didn't want a divorce but it was very important for her to get this tattoo. He didn't divorce her and her very large, red tattoo, while covered, represents her gratitude to red cardinals for saving her life so she could help others reach a new life through sobriety.

Every Christmas at the entry of the organization we would have a small Christmas tree along with other items of the season. On the Christmas tree was always a red cardinal. I always also have a red cardinal on my own Christmas tree in gratitude for it having saved the life of my dear friend.

Cinda Cash Walsh

Reflections on my Loving

Questions again: Who and what am I loving? How do the branches of Being translate into Loving? How are they impacted by principle? What are the passions that inform them?

A central branch of Being is principles. The principles by which I live – strong, grounded, rooted, remarkable. What are these principles that create my wilding path? I think them through, I feel them through. They need repeating and reinforcing daily.

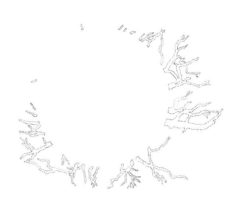

There are universal principles of honesty, generosity, unconditional love, self-responsibility and many more. And each of us, each wilding woman, has our own principles that we live by. Mine are reflected in the work I did on my quest around the old patterns of behaviour that blocked me and kept me stuck – guilt, appeasement, low self-esteem and the rest – so my work is to know what the principles are and to uphold them.

For example, I have a principle that has emerged from my work on guilt – to deal immediately with whatever I may have done that is wrong, and to refuse to pick up other people's responsibilities. I have a principle of appreciation – to look for the good that is behind what others say and do, to assume it, whether or not I can see it. And in doing so I find that the good appears, and our connection and collaboration strengthens. Our wilding work is to ask ourselves questions until we know what those principles are.

Beyond the principles, what are the passions? The passions that drive my wilding, my wilding life? My own passions are my family, my husband-lover, my friendships, my creativity, my health, this wilding women journey. These are the passions that guide me, that drive me. How do I keep them in balance, so that my art work, say, does not flourish at the expense of seeing my family? Or that my part of the wilding women journey does not overshadow my health, or my intimate relationships?

Between the LOVING circle and the DOING circle is a narrow ring, edged on the inside with a deep red cord, cross-stitched in green silk and outlined in black chain stitch. From its outer edge long sun-bursts of yellow and green silk thread, highlighted by fine ink lines, stretch outwards, with my own grandmother's black jet beads emphasising their rays. Written in green ink around the outer edge are the messages from the four directions, east, south, west and north. This is the threshold between inner and outer, the marue as it is called in Korean to describe the raised step between rooms that must be stepped over to move from one room in the house to the next. It holds everything I need for the journey.

DOING: The wilding way

What if.... this next circle is about how I act on a day-to-day level – what I say, what I do, how I do it?

Reflections on my DOING

Questions

This outermost ring, the small branches and twigs, is my Doing – the activities that make up my day-to-day life; the things I do to nurture and express my Being and my Loving. If I have a passion to make art images, what are the loving actions I must take to make this happen? What are the principles that will keep my artwork in balance with the rest of my life, and make sure it is nourished and honoured? If part of the central Being of my wilding woman journey is a loving and collaborative sharing, what is needed to make this safe and generous?

Grandmother Tree's branches reach the next circle, the Doing circle, still plain white leather, but as they cross this narrow band they cease being white and grow outwards towards the edge of the skin a cool greeny-blue. When I was working in industry, it was easy enough for people to come up with wishlists of vision statements, of values: 'Respect each other', 'Treat  everyone equally', 'Always work for the good of the organisation'. We called these the 'Motherhood and apple pie' statements, and challenged: 'What does this mean?' 'How does this translate into day-to-day behaviour?' 'What are the DBMs?' This meant 'Do By Monday' – what are the small things that you will do, the changes that you will make by the end of the week that will make a difference incrementally to your organisation, to your fellow workers, and to yourself?

The research question: Whaddaya mean by that? Is relevant here – the devil, as they say, is in the detail. If I couldn't ground an assertion firmly in the literature, in my research, then I was told: 'Go away and come back when you do know what you mean.' In an early seminar (we met three times a year) I was bandying the word syntax around, and when challenged couldn't come up with what I meant. Six months later, at the next seminar, I presented a single slide that built up a clear and cogent picture of exactly what I meant by syntax. It went on to form the core of my final dissertation.

Doing holds attention to detail, to how I do things, to what I am thinking and feeling when I do them. Doing is reflected in so many phrases and sayings: 'Handsome is as handsome does'; 'By their fruits shall you know them'; 'A single act is worth a million thoughts'.

Clean Sweep

Whilst she crouched on the floor,
Sweeping crumbs by the drawers
That her mother had left
The remains of digest.
She huffed and she blew,
Making anew, the red carpet.
She was tired and dimmed
And was wearing quite thin.
At the beck and call of her mother,
She had nursed,

She had fed,
She had clothed,
Her instead. She had lifted and
lowered
As no other.
She had cared well for the woman
Who had cared well for her.
And she frequently wished she had
Brothers.
She was passing out daily

In the quest to do good,
She was self pressurising
A slave to the 'should'.
But in that there were moments
She stood up empowered,
She spoke up for herself,
She spoke up quite loud
As if her own Ally,
She changed 'should' to 'would',
She stated her feelings,
She stated her words,
She was still being treated
Like a little girl
Taught to help, and always to care
For all those around her,
To love and to share
This was all very well,
She had kept up this act.
But on this occasion
Her mindset, it snapped.

Her mother's heart was better,
Her mother was new
But was taking advantage
Of all that she'd do.
Enjoying assistance and bossing
about,
Living through her daughter
And hardly ever going out.

She was depending too heavily,
And leaning too much

Taking for granted her daughter's
Loving touch.

Love and care should comprise
Of give and of take.
But on this day, she sensed
Resentment and some hate.
She vowed to stop,
Her work was done.
Nearly three years of moons
And suns.

She was angry,
She was shaking,
She was strength in the making.
She'd feel guilty,
She'd feel shame,
But she couldn't continue to play
This game.

And in time the mother moved out,
And the daughter let go.
The unravelling began, where
She went no one knows.
Off the rails for a while
But when it all played out
The mother got help with
Official clout.

She got her own flat,
Clean and bright and new.
Carers came in bringing

Food, providing glue.
She got helpful meds
That evened her out
Less ups and less downs.
And visitors about.
She was loved by many
She had many friends.
Their relationship mended
Revived and restored.

And the daughter learned
Her lesson, that she deserved
More.

More questions

When I look at the six main branches in my Being, I can see how each travels and transforms through the circles. When my creativity branch grows from my core Being into my Loving the questions are about the passion behind it; what is the subject of my creativity? What medium should I use for each piece of creativity – writing? (and if so, prose? poetry?) drawing? painting? sculpture? leatherwork? dance? What is the best way to communicate the passion behind the ideas, the drive behind the images and words? How can I best balance my creative work with my other loves – family, lover, health, adventure?

And as the creativity branch crosses through the transition ring from the Loving circle into the Doing circle, the questions are about how I use my skills, how I develop them, extend them. How do I make the time for my creative work, find and hold the space   physical, emotional, spiritual, mental – to carry out my creative work, how do I react when I find my hands getting hungry for making?

Doing is particular to each person, to each community. If one of the Being branches in a family is unconditional love, how does this translate into behaviour when things become difficult? In a family there are always times when things become difficult.

Grandmother Tree's branches become more irregular and uneven as they grow further from her central trunk. In some areas they are strong and chunky, while in others they are almost non-existent. Grandmother Tree grows in her own idiosyncratic way and teaches me that perfection is always imperfect; and that imperfection is always perfect.

Moon shadow

The outermost circle is the moon shadow. The light of the full moon during my quest felt as strong as the sun. The shadows it cast were inky black on the ground, which had turned silver. A poem by de la Mare captures so perfectly what I saw in the dead of night. It starts:

'Slowly, silently, now the moon/Walks
the night in her silver shoon/This way
and that she peers, and sees/Silver
birds upon silver trees.'

In my journal I wrote:

> *The moon shadow holds*
> *everything. It fuses the shadows of*
> *Grandmother Tree, the juniper bushes,*
> *my tent, the smaller plants; and I wonder*
> *if this is how my community is made? How*
> *everything, still separate, nevertheless merges under the moon?*

The individual moon-shadow shapes of this outer circle, I took from the shadows cast during the day by the sun on the ground and on the side of my tent. It was too cold at night to do anything other than notice and enjoy the moon shadow's density and opacity, and store up its features in my mind's eye for working on it in the morning.

Again in my journal:

> *This is indeed where the seeds of the Wilding Women stories are sown. Each*
> *story a part of the whole, and the whole strengthened by each individual; the*
> *magical connections between so many disparate lives, the threads that weave*
> *the greater story together, that co-create a community.*
>
> *Once upon a time...*

When these moon shadow shapes appeared on the map, I had no idea what they were or what they would become, but Grandmother Tree knew, and the map knew, and now – at last – I know that they are the journey, the circles, of wilding women.

Moon path

The ink splashes cut a path across all the circles. They remind me that life principles apply at all levels – in my being, in my loving, in my doing.

These are the desire lines, worn by the continuous treading of feet along a path that emerges as the feet tread it, that the feet tread as the path gets clearer. The desire lines on the map remind me of my emerging vision of circles of women across the world, laughing, supporting, learning, having fun, singing and dancing with life.

I wrote a Haiku recently:

Sun sinks, Moon rises

Laughing women dance, arms linked –

Earth turns on a smile

I had some large stone disc beads left over from a previous leather work, and found myself placing one of them on the black-cloth background just beyond the leather at the end of the ink splashes. This, I realise with a great lifting of heart, is what my teacher meant when she stood next to me at the end of my first quest, and pointed to the moon:

'Lasso the moon – the rope is your path'. The wilding map is complete.

My Story – Part I

STORY 20

"Light is easy to love. Show me your darkness." R. Queen

Standing in Jayne's office, I listened half-heartedly to her begging me to come along to The Journey workshop. Resistance turned to annoyance. Searching for a credible objection, I peered out the window through a horizontal gap in the slats and saw the words Brandon Block displayed in huge letters on a poster. Accustomed to reading signs from life, I startled, and then caught the cosmic joke and precision of the synchronicity! I told Jayne that something said I was meant to go.

Travel to the Brandon Bays workshop was itself a rather mythical quest, as sign after sign appeared en route: a total stranger gifting me a meaningful tarot card on the tube; a personal insignia spotted above a gate; and treasured winged beasts carved in stone at the entrance. My twenty-seven-year-old self gleefully embraced these early discoveries of the spiritual realm where everything felt imbued with the mystery.

Once inside in plush conference surroundings, I listened intently as we learned about Brandon's approach to accessing deep consciousness through body channels. Engaged and open, I delighted in the inputs and visualisations, but already dreaded the second day when we ourselves would practice the technique.

On day two, I found myself powerfully drawn to a very young man. The sense was mutual and we paired up, as was life's design. In a room of over 200 people it transpired that he was from France, a country I adore and whose language I speak fluently.

I practiced first, tuning in to discover the part of his body that might hold relevant information for releasing any unconscious blockage, which unattended might lead to more serious physical illness. The body intelligence guided us using inner visualisation to a deep, damaged looking root in a large back tooth. We sat for a time, waiting to see what it would reveal. But something inside said *go deeper*. Unsure whether to trust this knowing, I continued to wait, but the insistence and intensity grew, so I guided him to travel deeper down the root – where we were taken deep into the brain.

A dark, ominous-feeling cell cluster waited at the end of the long fibres, and he began to sob uncontrollably. 'What's happening?' I asked. He was back in a traumatic memory from early childhood: the moment he had found the body of his older brother who committed suicide in their home.

Without thought, I switched to his language. I heard his distraught child voice – unspoken words of grief, horror, despair, loneliness and regret. Helpful sentences formed in my mouth to be said, whilst all the time 'I' was watching, as if outside of the process. I understood that a greater intelligence was at work, attending to the tumour – administering healing with precision and 'I' was its willing instrument.

My Story – Part 2

*"Yea though I walk through the valley of the
shadow of death,
I will fear no evil." (Psalm 23:4)*

And then it was my turn. Still bewildered and in awe, I lay down hesitantly to begin the inner journey. So many years ago, it now feels like a distant dream.

I went down a staircase and was greeted at the doorway to the unconscious by the wise guide. He appeared as the film character Yoda and I burst into hysterical laughter, wondering whether to take any of this seriously. His incongruous apparition and my response masked the nature of what was to come.

Following the process, I came to a group of wise, loving supporters – some living, some dead. They all gathered in a circle. I noted my beloved maternal grandmother amongst them. Looking strangely solemn, they asked if I was ready.

Ready for what?

The wise guide led me to an enormous edifice: a gigantic tombstone the size of a tower. I stood in its long, dark shadow, which extinguished all light. He handed me a hammer-like tool and instructed me to smash the tombstone utterly and completely. I was to place each remnant into the blazing fire beside me, to be transformed by divine flames.

I just stood there paralysed, barely breathing. Powerless. Staring up at the enormous monument to death. It possessed me with its implacable indifference and its chill. I felt the presence of the murdered, and all the dead, and the vast industry of the Holocaust. My own visceral ambivalence to life was unmasked. Riven by resistance, terror, rage and guilt, I was fixed in its deathly gaze and unconscious bonds.

Words burst out of me: *Who will remember them and keep their memory sacred?*

I howled. I cursed. I fought, until eventually I had no fight left. Breaking up the edifice took the longest time. I was dimly aware that in the real world, four skilled hands had moved in to hold me by wrists and ankles, as tears drenched us.

When the flames had consumed every last remnant, Time and Space slowed down and stopped. Unearthly hands suspended me in the boundless empty, and I noticed two vast wings unfurling from my shoulders. They went on into infinity in either direction. And there was a light, which poured through my body. Emanating. Words began pouring from my lips. Sweet words. Praising words. Blessings on the people in the room... outside in the streets... in the city... it spread ever outwards, until the blessings covered the whole earth. I stayed there for hours, though only minutes in the real world.

Back in normal awareness, I was very much my usual self again. I had no conception of the inner and outer work that lay ahead, only that everything had changed. That's when the journey with unity and consciousness truly began. It is a forever work in progress!

CHAPTER TEN

Themes of life

The learning I have done with my teachers, in ceremonies and in my two quests, has woven patterns and themes across the years. Themes of the glories of Mother Earth - the trees, the birds, light, the weather with its wind and storms, its heat and cold.

The trees; the birds; light and spirit

Trees

'The trees are the first teachers'.

My medicine name – my ceremonial name – is WalksWithTrees. A medicine name is one that you chose, or more often that choses you, that somehow captures the essence and the best of who you are. Medicine names sometime arrive in a moment of clarity or inspiration, sometimes in a dream. Others, like mine, take much longer to emerge; it took at least a year before mine appeared.

I knew I had a deep love and affinity with trees, and I knew that with a lifetime of often frenetic activity, I needed their calm and slow pace. I tried out 'dancing' or reversing the order of words – TreeWalker or TreeDancer – I tried DancingTree, and other combinations. Eventually I simply held the intention of a medicine name that would keep me continually challenged and inspired, and stepped back from the tussle.

It was at a ceremony in England with David that the name WalksWithTrees settled. On the second morning, when we were speaking our names and intentions into the circle, I said, 'I am WalksWithTrees'. Immediately my teachers and the rest of the group shouted 'Ho!' and that was my medicine name declared and honoured.

People sometimes get it wrong, and it becomes WalkingWithTrees, or something stranger. A young man approached me at a ceremony in Sweden: 'Can I ask you a question?' 'Certainly,' I replied. 'Tell me,' he said. 'Why are you called WalksWithCheese? Is it about breakfast?'

WalksWithTrees keeps me on track, reminds me of the slow pace I need to stay focused, reminds me to be the best of myself at every moment. Being with the pinyon pines and juniper bushes on my quests kept me gently and firmly on track.

The trees bring gifts and blessings. Sitting working on the deerskin one afternoon, my eye is caught by a flutter of brown – another small butterfly? But no, there is another, and another, not butterflies but leaves, cottonwood leaves, whirling in the air about my head. But the nearest cottonwood trees are way down at the foot of the canyon, hundreds of feet down from the canyon rim, which is itself half a mile away from my quest site. Still they come, and the air is thick with them. They say that every falling leaf that you catch, or that even touches you, is a day of happiness in the year to come. I know I will be very blessed.

'I've never seen that before,' says my guide. 'That is very special.'

In my journal I wrote about the trees:

> The trees teach me manners. If I push through them, I get bashed on the shoulder.

> They teach me awareness and play. If I get solemn, I get a gentle knock on the hand. If I get distracted, a whack on my head; if I need to wake up out of a doze, a nudge on my shoulder.

They teach me about the Sacred Human – the 5 – in the five branches of a pinyon pine coming out of the ground on the edge of my first quest site. They formed an oval space where I would sit, and draw, and learn to listen.

They teach me to listen: 'Ask your guide for ribbons,' they said. Grandmother Tree told me she was coming home with me.

They teach me generosity – they welcome the insects and creatures and me into their shade.

They teach me to smile and to chat with my Tree Sisters.

They teach me gratitude. They so willingly give me shelter, and privacy for my bodily functions.

They teach me love – tough love and unconditional love.

They teach me guardianship – tree sentinels guard my site.

They teach me to be present: to slow to their pace.

Mary Oliver's poem *When I Am Among the Trees* sums up so much of what the trees are teaching me:

'" It's simple," they say, "and you too have come into the world to do this, to go easy, to be filled with light, and to shine."'

Birds

All through my quests and the days of preparation, I am aware of the birds. The birds bring me messages. Messages of blessing, of challenge, of warning, of wake-up, of laughter. They lead me across the land to hear my messages from the earth.

In my journal I write:

I AM HERE – with the birds.

Grandmother Tree is full of birds, all chirruping to each other, gently keeping an eye on me – or so it feels – and glad to be here, now. As I am.

I write:

Blessed birdsong.

There are many birds on my two quests; here I honour the ravens, the hummingbirds, and the pinyon jays.

Ravens patrol the air. They keep a watchful eye and rarely interfere. They warned me about a storm coming, and that I should get my tarpaulin sorted. They visited to bless me. Each day three ravens soared through the air above me, angling their wings towards me, calling out to each other, and checking up on me and my fellow seekers.

They observe me, they challenge me when I'm distracted; their presence reassures me. Waiting for the taxi to take me back to the airport, I start to get anxious about it being late. I'm all ready to launch into a projection where I miss the plane, when a raven wheels by, scolding me roundly, and I settle into enjoying the sun warming my back, treasuring the last glimpses of the canyon, and smiling at the chipmunks dashing back and forth under the trees. The taxi arrives.

Two pinyon jays in Grandmother Tree, chirruping to each other. And another one – two – three. And another one. The setting sun turns their breasts pink and gold. They fly in short dipping arabesques. They join each other, congregate, then fly off towards the sunset, dipping in concert, pink and gold together.

Hummingbirds visited me on my first quest. As I sat very still in the shade of a pinyon pine – a sister to Grandmother Tree – stitching deep red corals onto my leather buckskin, the hummingbirds would come and try to sip nectar from the beads. And when I wore my red checked shirt, a present from my beloved husband-lover, they came to my shoulder or my arm – always from my left side, my heart side – drawn by the colour. They blessed the space, my work, and my presence on their land.

My guide tells me the hummingbirds are messengers of light.

Light as Spirit, Spirit as Light

At the start of my first quest each seeker was invited to pick, without looking, a prayer scroll. The one I chose – that chose me – was:

I am a divine manifestation of the universe. Within every cell of my body, here and now, I am white light inside me. I am self-contained and pure light.

The hummingbirds started to visit the next day.

At the end of that quest, after my final night-ceremony, I was carefully putting the fire out, when suddenly there were lights all around me. In my journal I wrote:

Lights on the rocks, shimmering and shifting. Lights in the trees and in the sky. Lights moving and shimmering.

The lights were shaped almost like jellyfish, or a round cloth, They draped over the clumps of grasses, cacti and fungi on the ground, and floating in the air, and in the trees. Golden warm lights, about six inches across, depending on where they draped. Benevolent, detached, playful, just THERE, moving, flickering, pulsating. When I moved to pick up my prayer bag filled with prayer bundles, a bolt of light from inside the bag shot straight up into the air. White light and very powerful. My heart was full of awe, of wonder, of joy. Then I needed to wee, and when I came back from behind the tree, the lights were gone.

'They are the Spirit People,' said my guide. 'They can be seen,' she said, 'show themselves, to people who are open to them.' And my state of being at the end of my ceremony opened me up to them.

I reflected how they are both benign – floating, shimmering, shifting, beautiful – and naked raw power. The blast that came out of the prayer bag gave me a very strong and painful electric shock. All 'white light inside me'.

Then in my second quest, watching the sunrise each day, watching the light on the hills shift and change in the minutes before Father Sun arises in all his glory and amazement.

Watching the light pushing the shadow of my sundial round the hours.

Watching the light slowly glow on Pedernal.

Watching the moon rise.

Watching the stars and finding the Great Bear and the Little Bear and Cassiopeia, and Orion with his belt and sword and –

Oh glory! the North Star.

Falling in love again

STORY 21

Alban Berg's opera, Lulu, is one of the masterpieces of the early twentieth century.

Many years ago, there was a very special performance on TV from the Paris Opera. This would be the first time the third act of the opera would be performed. It had been known that an incomplete third act existed and now it had been completed and here it was, staged and on television. Lulu is that terribly dangerous character, a femme fatale, who attracts devotion and desire from both men and women, a fate which leads all to destruction. The two-act opera takes the audience through the descent of Lulu and her entourage into corruption and murder. Until now we were left wondering where her story would finally lead her and her troupe of besotted lovers. The third act would give us resolution, however terrible and tragic that might be.

I was visiting my parents and they had invited me to go with them for dinner with friends of theirs I did not know. I explained how I had seen the opera twice in its incomplete form and was really excited to see the completed version conducted and sung by world-class artists and would they mind if I stayed at home to watch.

Staying with my parents was never easy or relaxing. Usually by day three my mother had taken to her bed of an afternoon, and I had found some way to get out for a break. My father just stayed in a mild state of confusion, always supportive of his wife as mother and daughter set each other off. Underneath our social meetings were mistrust on my side, and, I think, jealousy and competition on hers. As an adult I didn't like her very much, as a child she had confused me.

I sat on the floor glued to the unfolding production from Paris. It was overwhelming, and sitting only four foot away from the screen, all embracing. As the third act began, my parents returned from their dinner. I indicated that this was it... the moment I had been waiting for and went back to the screen, irritated by their presence but determined not to let it distract. They stood behind me, watching. As soon as it became clear that Lulu, now a prostitute, was going off with a client, my father, a glorious prude, tut tutted and bid us good night. He left. The act continued and the three or four now desperate members of Lulu's troupe revealed the tragedy of their lives, full of longing and despair.

I glanced round at my mother. She was transfixed. Standing, watching the television, she was completely taken into the unfolding opera. She was totally open to the experience of the story, there were tears in her eyes as there were in mine. I saw her and knew I could truly love this woman. I fell in love with her as a woman and loved her again as my mother. From then on, I was able to be myself with her, and drop my defensive barriers. For the remaining ten years of her life, we could meet and value each other.

Re-entry

At the end of the week, I pack up my campsite, and observe one of the fundamental precepts of living with the land – leave no trace. I make sure there is nothing – no scrap of rubbish, obviously, but more than that, no footprint in the dust, no half-demolished stone altar, no guide-stone or significant feather – nothing that indicates any human has ever been in this place. I put all my camping gear into the one bag (it fits this time) beyond the boundary of my quest site, find a bushy twig and walk backwards off the land sweeping out my footsteps as I go. But first I say my goodbyes and thank-yous to Pedernal, sacred mountain, and to Grandmother Tree. Pedernal is brusque: 'You know what to do, get on with it.' I say to Grandmother Tree, 'I shall miss you.' 'Oh no you won't,' she replies. 'I'm coming with you.'

And so she did – she hangs in our hallway in all her magnificence and glory and continuous reminder that this work – writing this book, discovering what is wilding, living it, and as the months progress, taking the wilding idea out into the world – is my work. Mine to do.

The first thing to do is to make the space and the time to do the wilding work.

My guide's two key questions are resonating as I think through the many things I am engaged with: writing two academic papers with colleagues, on the steering groups of two research projects, the advisory groups of two more, to say nothing of running a support group and supporting research interest groups in the Parkinson's community. I go through the list interrogating each one: Does this activity grow corn? Answer in almost every case: Yes. Is it mine to do? Answer in nearly every case: No. There are many other people who could do this as well as and probably better than me. I make phone calls, write emails, have meetings, and miraculously (or so it feels – there's nothing miraculous about it at all, it's just putting aside

the old habit of saying 'yes' because of not wanting to disappoint people)
my time frees up and I can focus on the things I need to focus on, like my
exercise regime, and my art in the studio, and this wilding work.

It does grow corn. And it is mine to do.

So, packed up and leaving no trace, I come off the land and meet up with
the other seekers. We share moments from our quests – I tell the gathering
how Mother Earth held me on her breast and cradled me to sleep. Then
we visit hot mineral springs, to soak away the dust and the week's grime.
Rupert Brooks in his poem *The Great Lover*, talks of the benison, the
physical blessing, of hot water. Ah, yes.

The place is quiet, people speak softly, voices muted, and under it all, the
sound of the water bubbling up as it has done for hundreds of thousands
of years, flowing to the surface from its volcanic aquifers. The night falls
and the stars come out; the pools steam gently. I lie, held by the water,
marvelling at the stars, and the generosity of the earth – such gifts. I
am in awe. I pay attention to each tiny detail, to the huge over-arching
pattern of life, and to everything in between. To the pebbles under my
bare feet, and the red cliff towering above the pool I float in; to the tiny
lights illuminating the pathways and the blaze of stars across the sky; to
the feel of the hot water on my body, and the cool of the night air on my
face as the temperature drops towards zero again. To the smell of the
minerals in the water – iron, arsenic, soda, lithia – and the tantalising
whiff of dinner drifting from the restaurant. I pay attention to the
warmth of my feelings for my fellow seekers on the quest, our helpers,
and for my guide.

The next day I fly home. I barely need the plane.

Mind you, going through security a courteous Homeland Security guard
asks me to 'Step aside please, Ma'am'. I have left a Leatherman knife in
the foot of my carry-on baggage. The guard decides I am no threat, even

offering to find my hold baggage and put the knife in it for me. I foresee lost baggage, missed planes, palaver, and thank him kindly, but no.

I sleep most of the way home.

My Diagnosis –
in Words....and Music?

STORY 22

When I was given the diagnosis of Parkinson's at the age
of fifty-nine, I felt that doors were closing,
shutting out the light.

I'd taken a new job as an advisory teacher and thought I was safe till I was sixty-five. But no. That neurologist said he'd see me in a year, and in that time my world would be changed irreparably.

I was despondent and thought it unfair. Unfair came eighteen months later when I had surgery to remove my gall bladder. And unfair again when a simple pre-op X-ray showed something. On Christmas Eve I was informed that I had a tumour on my lung and in six weeks I'd have it removed with the lower lobe of my right lung.

How bad could it get?

I took a look at myself. I had to see what I could do, and more importantly, what I could do to help others. I'd already joined the local branch of Parkinson's UK and valued the support that was being freely given to me. So I planned to do a skydive – yes... you heard me – a skydive. The experience was one of fear, anxiety, exhilaration and excitement. The sponsorship raised £5000.

From then on, I worked on being positive and have tried to help fellow members to look at their own lives positively. I work hard to provide an interesting programme for members and have created a team who offer different skills and expertise, but all aimed at giving the best we can for our members.

Out of the blue I heard from Open University that they were offering me an Honorary Master's Degree for Public Service. In April 2018 I was treated with utmost respect when I collected my degree. I've since been awarded two further Honorary Doctor Degrees, and I am pleased the Parkinson's community is recognised in this way.

Now, looking back – is every door closed to me? No! New doors have opened and welcomed me in. If I can do it I'm sure others could too. Helping is a phone call, an email, a listening ear and most of all a cheery 'hello' with a smile.

Now, instead of feeling despondent when I wake up each day, I think: "I'm feeling GOOOOD!"

CHAPTER ELEVEN

Back in the world

'This is the beginning year of the era of wilding women.' Soo Young Lee, Wilding Woman.

Back home I now have the task of writing about wilding - of articulating the idea, the concept, the practice, and sending it out into the world to do its work. 'This is important,' said my teacher. 'Women need this.'

In her *Recollections of my Non-existence* Rebecca Solnit imagines a world without misogyny and the fear and pain it engenders:

'I suspect [the earth] would be dazzlingly alive and that a joyous confidence now rare would be so common, and a weight would be taken off half the population that has made many other things more difficult to impossible.'

My teacher says:

'There is something women are called to be and do in this time of the world. What is that... what is the call? If we are not on the wilding path, we cannot be free to show up in the way we are needed now...

to usher in peace;

to create a new society;

to speak truth that might be uncomfortable;

to birth something new in the world;

to create a collective ... where all our voices are heard;

to dream;

and we need the wilding path to walk... so we can show up... in the power of woman!'

Wilding, I am beginning to deeply understand, isn't mine. It came from the land, not from me. I was the person there with the readiness to hear it, to accept it and to carry it out. I take a deep breath...

Once upon a time...

Being, loving, doing...

Spaces for feeling alive

I'm sitting in the bay window of David's and my apartment in central Edinburgh, looking out onto the street. Our front windows directly face the windows of the flats opposite, but the road is wide, and they don't feel intrusive. I see them – and any passers-by – through a partial screen of my window box flowers: in spring, pale creamy-coloured daffodils and delicate narcissus, crimson cyclamen, grape hyacinths – muscari, a wonderful name – tiny jewel-like irises, a hellebore, and lavender; in summer, assorted geraniums and pelargoniums, deep blue lobelia, paler calendula – a riot of unplanned plantings. I had had visions of beautifully manicured window boxes rich in trailing petunias and variegated nasturtiums, but instead they are filled by the waifs and strays of the local flower shops' 'reduced' boxes. And none the worse for that – the bees love them.

Inside there are cut flowers by season – red parrot tulips with their fringe of green ruffles, sweet-smelling many-headed narcissus, alstroemeria and roses – and pot plants: the vigorous leafy remains of three astonishing amaryllis, a deep purple and a deep red primula that were presents for my birthday, a peace plant, and a succulent that will – I hope – survive my ministrations. (It didn't.) By and large I'm not good with pot plants. The peace plant is a surprising exception: a gift from a cherished colleague at the end of a wonderful collaboration, it has flourished through drought and neglect and over-attention from grandchildren. I water it and even remember to feed it from time to time. It responds by giving me delicate greeny-white lily-shaped flowers and doubling in size every two years – it now needs its third repotting.

In March each year on my birthday, the sun lifts above the rooftop opposite and shines directly into the apartment all day: the greatest gift possible. As I sit in the bay window, I have my laptop on my knee and am writing this book.

The ecology of wilding

The physical space we occupy makes such a difference to how we feel and act within it.

Virginia Woolf knew that, in order to write, a woman needed a room of her own (a space where she would not be interrupted) and £500 of unearned income a year – that is, financial independence. £500 a year, in 1929, was not a fortune, but it was enough to live in comfort, not having to worry about paying the rent, or where the next meal would be coming from.

My bay window is my den, my room of my own; and my modest retirement pension is my £500 a year.

In the 1970s, the architect and academic, Christopher Alexander sent his university students out across the world to ask people: 'What kind of physical space makes you feel most alive?' Analysing the answers, they identified 153 'patterns', from the largest, a regional scale of hundreds of square miles, all the way to the smallest – tiny things that made a big difference, like growing herbs between paving stones on a garden path or positioning a lamp above an easy chair to create a pool of light for private reading. These patterns, when used in architecture and in ordering a private or public space, create a sense of calm, of wellbeing, of 'feeling most alive'.

One pattern I find particularly sympathetic describes a space between our public and private worlds; an elision of inside and outside, a transition space, between street and home. The traditional front porch in the US South with its rocking chair or porch swing; a hidden courtyard in a busy Parisian back street. A friend lives in Paris on such a street – noisy, populous, occasionally threatening. But the moment you step through the small door set in a large metal gate everything changes. You are in a courtyard filled with pots of flowering shrubs, the street noise fades and you feel safe and relaxed and ready for the climb up the stairs to her apartment.

Visiting a friend in Marrakesh's Medina, arriving at midnight, I stepped from the noise and crush of the derbs, the Medina's narrow lanes, through a small wooden gate set into a much larger one, then into a short, angled corridor that led to a magical space surrounded by balconies running round three sides of a square courtyard. Open to the sky, the roof was the stars. This was another atom of delight: standing, open-mouthed, looking up and up, totally beyond words.

Stories, especially children's stories, often use the device of the transition space, the gateway between worlds: Alice falling down the rabbit hole or stepping through the looking glass; the children discovering Narnia through the back of their great-uncle's wardrobe; Dr Who's Tardis in a British police box; Harry Potter's Platform 9 ¾ at King's Cross station for the Hogwarts Express. Each a portal between the everyday and the magical and mysterious.

In Edinburgh some of the New Town tenement houses have a wide stoop (the Scots word for the front step) and of a summer evening it becomes another transition space, when the inhabitants set out chairs, even small tables, and with a glass of wine watch the world going by. Our own stoop isn't wide enough to accommodate chairs or even a narrow bench, so I have put slender planters to create a liminal space from the pavement to the front door. Coming in from the street I pass a clematis (in summer a riot of extravagant white flowers), lobelia, lavender and ivy. Then through the street door into our shared tenement staircase. Until recently the walls were painted a dark and gloomy maroon, and every time I entered my heart sank. It is now celadon, palest greeny blue, which lifts the spirits. The light streams down from the cupola at the top of the stairs, and the bannisters, repainted black, stand out in their full late-Victorian detail. I hang plants from the curve of the handrails, further bringing the outside in; coming home, the space welcomes me in from the street, and going out, sends me into the world with a smile.

All this is my ecology, crucial in supporting my creativity and wellbeing, and – back to Christopher Alexander – making me 'feel alive'. I discover that the word 'ecology' comes from the ancient Greek word for house.

An invitation: Your wilding ecology

What do you have already in your wilding ecology?

Are you full of gratitude for it?

What is still needed?

How can you figure out what needs to happen – what to do, who to speak with, where to find what is needed?

I have everything I need in order to write – the space, the time, the passion. The first part of this book – the story of the quest and the arrival of the wilding concept – is complete. And now I don't know how to take the story forward.

I'm stuck.

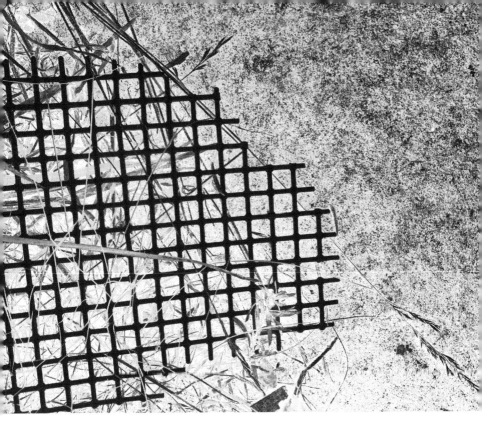

When my life tipped (1)

*I was twenty-eight, and six months pregnant. In a
phone call one day I learned that my grandmother
had cancer. I still remember the tremor that
passed across my already rounded belly, like a
premonition of a future full of uncertainty.*

As often as I could I went with my grandmother to her many obligatory chemotherapy sessions. Each week she left for the hospital by train, returning home the next day. She was increasingly exhausted but held on to her self-determination. Week by week, her hair falling out, her skin pallid and withered, she never lost her sense of humour and her joie de vivre. I was torn between the huge happiness of soon welcoming my first child and an infinite sadness in watching my grandmother slowly fade away.

Birth of my son, great joy and maternal happiness. After long months of suffering, my grandmother's treatment was stopped: it was not managing to heal her, and the cancer had metastasised everywhere.

At the same time, such is the sudden and invasive quality of the illness, I learned that I also had cancer – of the thyroid. 'A friendly cancer!' said the surgeon. Day after day I looked after my son, I carried on living, but I believed my days were numbered. Although I had no symptoms I felt as if my body had betrayed me, felt continuously as if my life was inexorably slipping away, that I would certainly die. Coming round from the operation, I became aware of the room I shared with two other people, I heard the nurses' voices, the noises of the trolleys squeaking across the floor, and I was astonished to be still there, still alive. One more month of treatment and the doctors told me I was clear of the whole business.

Slowly and gently, I stepped back into my life, re-establishing the contact with my son that I had to some extent lost. He must have been asking himself what kind of sad world he had landed in. My grandmother went into a hospice, and my visits to her tore me apart a little more each time. One day she said to me, 'One life arrives, another departs.' But I did not want to accept that she would soon be leaving.

As the visits followed, she no could longer sit up, then could no longer speak, then could no longer see, then no longer anything. She appeared to be sleeping, in a kind of pre-death coma. I gave up these visits, they were too sad. The day I started a new job, I learned that she had died in the night. I decided that despite everything despair had not won and that I would emerge from it for my son, to show him, to demonstrate that life could also be joyful, happy, light.

The memory of this time with its intense and conflicting emotions remains a forceful tipping-point moment between my status as a young woman, daughter and granddaughter, and that of a young mother. This ordeal had nevertheless taught me to immerse myself in each new day, in each small happiness offered, in each encounter and in the pleasure there is in simply being alive.

A time of gifts

One of the extraordinary things I have found about this wilding journey is that whatever is needed, arrives when it is needed. There were no places left on the October quest when I applied, but a space opened up for me. During the quest itself, the wilding concept emerged along with the challenge of getting it out into the world. And now in the writing of it, and making art around it, I am continually showered with gifts. Not always comfortable gifts, or gifts I wanted and had asked for, but always gifts I needed, that wilding needed.

As they say, the universe is not limited by my lack of imagination.

Or skill.

I wrote the first draft of the first part of this book in the first three months after returning from the quest. With Catherine, a long-time friend and wilding woman, I spent three days in a cottage deep in the hills of Highland Perthshire, both of us there to work on, and to share, our respective writings. She challenged things I had taken for granted, queried my assumptions, and was – as a good critical friend should be – completely honest about her personal and professional reactions to what I was writing, how I was writing it, and what she, as a reader, was taking from it – or not.

What I was taking from it was: my writing needed a lot of work.

Then the 2020 Covid-19 pandemic happened. It was, as Dickens says at the start of *A Tale of Two Cities*, the best of times, it was the worst of times. Within the bubble of isolation it became, for me, extraordinarily creative. The slender thread of internet wove itself into and around my life, connecting and inspiring, and bringing gifts that arrived unexpectedly from nowhere and everywhere; gifts that opened up my thinking, expanded my experience and were exactly what I needed to take the wilding idea forward. Or more precisely, exactly what the wilding idea needed to move where and how it needed to move.

And what was needed above all else was help with my writing. Cue serendipity...

A gift towards writing

Two weeks into lockdown an email arrived from The Festival of Audacious Women, a group of, yes, audacious women who each year put on a week of workshops and lectures challenging women to 'do what you always wished you dared'. They were offering Write to Remember, an online course about (how perfect!) memoir writing. I joined, and learned about shaping the trajectory of a story, managing language, phrasing and vocabulary, and using the six Ws : what, who, when, where, why and – most important of all – wisdom.

The first five of the Ws are self-evident, but it is the last, wisdom, that brings a memoir to life, that makes it worth reading. What have I learned from my life? From reflecting on my life? How have I changed, matured, transformed over the years? As Kierkegaard said: 'Life can only be understood backwards; but it must be lived forwards.' I am beginning to understand the blessing of having lived long enough to understand how to live, the blessing of my quest work in recognising the patterns in my behaviour that held me back, and in understanding that I can call forward my guardians, those magical beings whose energy shifted from destructive to powerfully beneficial.

The discipline of writing something every day and reading it first thing in the morning to the group and to Sarah, the tutor, for feedback and critique, gave me a sense of how a daily structure gets writing done. I learned from the group's critiques of my writing; and the insights I gained listening to others' writing, the discussions of how they wrote, how they expressed their ideas, thoughts and feelings, how the narrative pulled them along, gave me a lively appreciation of the extraordinarily wide range of possible approaches to writing.

By the end of the course, I had written a short piece that informed the first part of this book, and within another two weeks I had sent Sarah the revised (and re-revised and re-re-revised) two thousand words that I had read out to Catherine at the cottage. Sarah's critique on top of Catherine's reading was invaluable – my writing was tightening, improving.

And I still didn't know how to take the story, the wilding concept, forward.

When my life tipped (2)

Looking back on it now, I see my life as held in place behind an immense dam. Over time the water upstream got so heavy that cracks had started to appear. Day by day small stones fell out and rolled to the ground, the water began to seep out, to try to escape.

One day in the street it swept over me: a storm broke. Exchange of telephone numbers, and we met again a few days later in a café. His kindness was apparent in his smiling blue eyes, his large hands, and his low, almost hesitant voice. I allowed myself to fall in love, and the dam gave way, literally exploding. The water that had been held back so long flooded out, leaving me with an immense feeling of lightness and a happiness as powerful as it was unexpected.

Oppression, verbal violence and silence had been so much part of my previous life that I could not imagine any other way of living. To all outward appearances we were a close and happy family, it is true, but deep inside me the drops of water were gathering. I swallowed the blame, the contempt and the malice, powerless to challenge the rules that had been set. I knew well that things were no longer working, but I could not manage to put my thoughts into words, far less imagine that another life could be possible. After the event I realised just how much I had felt isolated, oppressed – I found it difficult sometimes even to breathe without making the connection between my family duties and my professional ones; both, certainly, performed satisfactorily, but embedded in a schedule with every minute accounted for and with no space to think or to breathe – none.

Exhausted also by having to face so much opposition to asserting the value of my own identity, have my voice and my needs heard, needs which to him seemed out of place, naïve, unthinking, even a waste of time: 'Why bother tiring yourself out baking bread when there is a bakery round the corner?'

Exhausted too by dragging this responsibility, too heavy for me, this contrary force which too often prevented me from moving forward. It was only through being brutal that I was able to break free of this possessive, jealous man, who – even today after five years apart – continues to verbally harass me. But I stand firm.

I have since learned what it is to live freely – and it is like a rebirth.

Breaking my old habits, my conditioning and my old beliefs, attachments and fetters, I am able to welcome all the possible ways there are to (re)discover myself. 'Having always been the person that I am and being so different from the person that I was.'

(Samuel Becket *Oh les Beaux Jours* 1963) I found the space to give free rein to my creativity, to enjoy myself, under the gaze of a loving and fun-loving man. And I laugh – and it is the very best of therapies!

Gifts of space, of time, of making images

We have a key to a private garden nearby, and during the Covid-19
lockdown went there every day for our permitted exercise hour. Feeling
like Oscar Wilde's *The Selfish Giant* who wouldn't let anyone, especially
children, into his garden, we opened a half-hidden gate and stepped into
eleven acres of paradise. I found a sheltered bench and started to draw. The
weather was perfect – warm and sunny, light breeze, not too hot, settled
from one day to the next. I got out my summer clothes and put away
my winter jerseys, completely seduced by the belief that it would last all
summer. (It didn't – this is Scotland.)

Each day we went to the garden, and I drew. I drew the trees that enclosed
the garden and watched with delight as the leaves slowly unfurled into
what the poet Moya Cannon calls 'the tree's great symphony of leaf'. I drew
the paths that wound through the trees and out beyond them. I drew the
far horizon of the sea, just visible through the treetops, and the looming
bulk of Arthur's Seat, increasingly hidden behind the new foliage. I drew
the sweep of the bank, and the breadth of the central lawn; the twists of
trunk and branch, the trellising of small branches. I became intimately
aware of the differing bone structures of holly and beech, of sycamore
and hornbeam, of horse chestnut and hawthorn, and how they fractalled
outwards and upwards, as Grandmother Tree does. I watched how they
spoke to each other, the conversations they held as they leaned into each
other, gently breathing in concert with the wind.

This time also was time out of time – I was back in the Kairos time of my quest when time became fluid, and I had found myself swimming in it. For the first time in my life, I closely observed the spring. Day by day there were new spring flowers in the garden; the snowdrops had already given way to drifts of white, yellow and purple crocuses by mid-March, and now the narcissus and daffodils were flowering. The muscari followed, and a small patch of fritillaries with their snakeskin patterned heads, some white, some purple-brown, then the primroses thick upon one of the banks under the beech trees, smelling as sweet as the narcissus. Bluebells and more daffodils and then the wonder of the magnolias and cherry blossom. Kairos time slowed my perception as it had done in New Mexico. As in John Montague's poem, I watched 'at perception's pace' as the spring unfolded in slow-motion. My steps and thoughts slowed to match, and the only thing that retained its pace was my mark-making – the urgency to complete a drawing in a single hour drove my hand and the inks across the paper. Ideas for a larger piece of work gradually emerged as I brought the drawings together and explored how I might express how the garden held and sheltered me and the others who used it. I started to create a composite work that I worked on in the makeshift studio I had set up at home.

Then an unexpected email, out of the blue, from Out of the Blue, the company who manage the studio spaces where, in normal times, I'm based, gave my work an immediate focus and direction. They were producing a zine – a small informal one-off magazine –inviting artwork that reflected how different studio artists were dealing with this lockdown. Would I be interested in contributing? Yes, of course. I worked with printouts of my drawings, collaging, drawing and writing on the piece, adding words as image and words as meaning. As I worked within the very restricted form of an A4 sheet of paper, the limitations – as they so often do – pushed my thinking and practice in new directions.

And with the zine piece, another leatherwork was born.

I find, as with the Grandmother Tree wilding map, that mark-making, sewing, embroidering, shaping the image on the leather taps deep into my creative unconscious; as the image grows, so does the writing. I hadn't initially thought of the leatherwork as being part of exploring the wilding, but the trees' conversations, the paths between the trees leading into unexplored spaces, take me back to the quest land: the ink and beading slicing diagonally across the centre are the wilding path, and the cool grey circle at the top left is the moon. 'Lasso the moon, the rope is your path...'

The work goes through many iterations over the next year as many different ideas and feelings emerge and fade and return. It becomes over-thought and complicated, and finally – finally – it tells me what it needs. Trust the process. I have just seen a heron flying over the houses opposite.

CHAPTER TWELVE

The gift of ideas

An extraordinary gift arrived from my teacher,
written from New Mexico on the Spring Equinox
with snow on the ground and a bright blue sky.

Getting unstuck

I had already sent an early draft to my teacher for comments and asking for suggestions on the direction the story might take.

She replied to my questions with: 'What if...'

What if the woman in the fairy tale meets other women on the path who ask her a question or tell her a tale, and she mirrors back to them how to find their own way on their wilding path... and this comes from the parts of her that understand (since she experienced something similar) but also who she is now?

What if one day she looks around from the top of the Grandmother Tree and sees so many young women there in the realm – walking on their own wilding paths?

What if... became the next part – this part – of the wilding journey.

By now I was realising that if I wrote the wilding book single-handedly it would be limited by my own experience, and broad as that may be, it is very partial. What if... opens up my thinking, and my guardians of Inspiration, of Abundance and of Connection step forward.

What if the wilding book contained many stories, not just mine?

So I ask two close women friends if they would each write a short piece about a time in their life when something shifted, when they truly saw their life and that new seeing became their reality. They do, and their stories are powerful and moving, both very different, both adding richness and depth to the emerging book. I'm finally learning to trust the power of collaboration.

I start to get a sense of how the world, in Rebecca Solnit's words, could 'be dazzlingly alive [and] a joyous confidence now rare would be so common'.

Gifts of connection and dance and friendship

Then, the next gift arrived.

Following a good friend's advice, I had made a sensible decision not to look at any kind of screen after ten in the evening, so that I could get a full and restful night's sleep. So here I was, playing solitaire on my laptop at eleven o'clock at night, feeling guilty. Just checking emails before switching everything off, there was one that I couldn't identify – should I delete it unread? Was it phishing? I took a gamble, and read:

Let's make stuff: 1:59

Everyone knows Andy Warhol and his famous fifteen minutes of fame, but are you familiar with Eun Me Ahn and her 1'59? With this project, the iconic South Korean choreographer offers thirty to forty amateurs, from all ages and backgrounds, from all over the world to create their own video work and shine online for one minute and fifty-nine seconds.

The email explained that 1:59 is the average attention span before people move from one internet video platform to another; it detailed the free online workshops that would support the video-making, and – the clincher – that I had to be an amateur performer and between 16 and 122 years old.

How could I resist? So, before any second thoughts could creep in, I wrote back and applied. And within three days received: *Anyohaseo!*

Anyohaseo is Korean for hello, bonjour, hola, Guten Tag, bom dia... But it is also Korean for goodbye, au revoir, ciao, Tschüß, adios... For now, it's hello and now let's dance!

The gifts arrived thick and fast.

In Zoom-based workshops run by Clint Lutes, the artistic coordinator, by Eun Me Ahn, and by others from Europe and Israel and America I learned how to dance within the frame of the screen – computer or film – and how to subvert the screen's boundaries. I learned that dance was more than dance; it was conversation and discussion and argument and telling jokes and laughing together. I learned how to get to know someone deeply whom I had never met and most likely never will. For a full three minutes a woman a thousand miles away and I looked into each other's eyes, respectfully, gently, and knew by the end of it a deep reciprocally trusting connection. I laughed at physical jokes played to music; I danced intimately with women in France, or Copenhagen, or Seattle or Seoul, sharing movements and responding to how they felt, how I felt, so many hundreds or thousands of miles away.

Memories

STORY 25

*I've been pondering 'wilding' and I think it is an
excellent word for females discovering/re-finding that
part of their female selves, (perhaps in comparing
behaviours and instincts with what a male is?) What
is it to be female without reconditioning from parents
and from society? And is the real female any different
from male? For me the true female is feral in nature
and something else that I can't put into words.*

A memory

When I was about ten years old, I was on holiday with my mum. We went to visit her old friends in Shropshire. Her friend had four sons of various ages. We were playing in the garden with wrapping paper still in their rolls and hitting each other with them, and one of the boys said I wasn't 'hitting hard enough'. The thought came to me: 'yes, that's right, because I didn't want to hurt you'. His words gave me permission to let go of this assumption that he would be hurt and 'released' the strength and determination and intent I wasn't using. The boy then got upset with me because I did start to hurt him in the play. He went back inside the house. I don't remember what his other brothers were doing. When he left, I felt almost ashamed and feared I would make my mum displeased with me and then a scolding would follow.

Second memory

One of these photographs showed me as a toothless seven-year-old standing with two of my female school friends. It was summer, the end of school term. I was wearing a dress and my two school friends wore a t-shirt with shorts or trousers. In the picture I am grinning and so is my school friend next to me, each showing the huge gap between our two incisors. The school friend on the end was not smiling as huge as we were. I believe in that moment, I felt a connection, a bond, a camaraderie, a moment of acceptance, a fluttering of exhilaration with my school friend because there was no shame in having no two front teeth, because our toothlessness was being celebrated with the act of us posing for a photograph, because in that period of time this toothless school friend was the only one who had something the same as me. I was not alone.

Third memory

As pre-teen I was abused by a family member. The abuse only happened once. There are times when events seem out of a person's power to control, that an individual has no choice but to comply, to

212

play dumb and hope the moment will soon pass. After feeling that something was not right, that what was happening to me was not appropriate, a voice, my own voice in my mind spoke loudly, clearly and calmly, labelled what was transpiring, that this was abuse – I was being abused. In this moment of acknowledgement my mind voice came up with a number of options for actions, and listed consequences to these actions. I was afraid of what may happen if I acted on my thoughts, but I could not let myself continue being in that state. I physically removed myself from the environment, from having my spirit and body broken. I saved myself from further damage. I became my own protector. As an adult looking back, I was a quite a powerful twelve-year-old.

More gifts of connection and dance and friendship

We started to share histories and personal stories; beginning to understand a little about how each other saw the world. One of the younger dancers – in her thirties – said how much she was enjoying – and amazed to be enjoying – collaborating with people so very much older than she was. 'I don't meet many older people in my life,' she said. 'And this is really interesting.'

I copied the dance movements of one of the few men in the group, glimpsing what it felt like to move as a man. And the videos, all thirty-one of them, each 1:59 long, showed yet another aspect of each of us.

Making the video – I'd never done anything like this before – was huge fun; one glorious sunlit evening David filmed me moving and dancing in the garden, weaving in and out of the trees, wearing my favourite flowery summer skirt.

Editing the video was totally absorbing. I choreographed the piece using abstract images – one for the words I wanted to speak, one for the movements and shape of the piece. My oldest son talked me through the editing; how to add still photographs, background sound and special effects. For the soundtrack I recorded the evening blackbird song, and got permission from Mugen Taiko, my teachers of Japanese drumming, to use a clip from one of their professional performances. The birdsong, the drumming and my spoken words wove the story together, along with the film of my dance and some photographs of the quest land.

But the most important gift was the gift of connection and friendship with the other participants, and the knowledge that it could be fostered virtually. We had never met face to face, and are unlikely to, and yet the openness and trust that the eight weeks of 1'59 created was remarkable. And once again the universe had gifted what wilding needed – yet more remarkable women.

I now had gifts that honed my writing skills, challenged and extended my image-making, gave me time and space, sparked ideas, and grew connection, dance and friendship.

I now had a strong sense of a collaborative process in building the book.

I now had the inkling of an idea about how wilding was going to move out into the world to do its work.

An invitation: Getting unstuck

What do you do to get unstuck? What might you try?

Are you good at accepting the gifts that arrive for you? Can you find joy in the gifts, even (especially) when they are not what you thought you wanted.

CHAPTER THIRTEEN

The heart of wilding

At the heart of wilding is the moment when I – when any woman – sees her life, her situation, her truth, clearly and without filters. This seeing can never be unseen. Reminding myself of what Minna Salami says: 'there are realizations from which you can never return, light-bulb moments that shape your destiny by revealing the constellations of your behaviour.'

The wilding process

The What if... idea grows, and I find that there are many more women – from many different countries – willing to think, to feel, to share their stories with each other, and with the world. The stories start to arrive, and they are exciting and varied and deeply personal. There is a hunger, an appetite, to write these stories, to reflect and remember, to choose and to share.

'Encore merci à toi de nous offrir la possibilité d'écrire ces épisodes de nos vies de femmes.' (Again, my thanks to you for giving us the chance to write about these episodes in our lives as women.) Cedissia

I ask whether the women would like to meet each other, and so we come together as a group, virtually. In a single magical hour we start to grow trust and confidence in each other and in ourselves, and to write more stories. And this conversation turns into the first of many.

The Mannequin

STORY 26

I'm auntie woman I took out your
womb, it's a mystery.
I took out your womb in the night
when you were sleeping
And in doing so I took out your
femininity too.
You have to understand you cannot
have a man now, Sophia.

My femininity closed up on me,
then I could not express joy or fear,
but still felt the burning knife
as I wanted to go up a gear with
Jack inside me
telling me what to do.

Don't go here! The knife asked me
not to move
so I turned into a mannequin, in a
shop window,
nothing between my legs except
thin air.

I stared straight ahead as they
dressed me in unisex wear
but inside I was in despair.

My eyes could not shut tight as
people started at me,
right in between my legs, to decide
for themselves my gender.

With head shaven, I looked like a
man alright.
But two hard lumps on my chest
were of the feminine type.
I wore khaki jeans and a sweatshirt,
something for the outdoors type.
But inside I was a woman, waiting
to be loved by a man and to be free.
And then one day Jack came my
way,
he went inside the shop and asked
for the mannequin, not the clothes.
He took me home that night.

My movements were not stiff but
subtle
and my eyelids began to open and
close on their own.

I could feel my heart beating again
like it did once before,
the cracks in my face turned into
folds of skin,
I was becoming more human from
within.

I would sit on a rainbow one day
again with him.

And someday that rainbow will
come again.

Mannequins can't think or feel for themselves, or so you think.
And of course, if you define them from within,
a hard shell will grow around them.
But some mannequins are meant to be born human.
The definition of one locks one into positions.
For he is the man within me,
returning me to me, returning me to him.

For the mannequin in the window stares no more,
for her eyes blink with the rain on her face.

You know, for I was a child and not a robot to begin with
until auntie woman took out my womb.
I can still feel the knife as she sliced me from end to end
for I can't have children now, but Jack doesn't care.

I'm not a mannequin for all to see,
so don't define me as one without emotion,
for my emotions are like the sea and the ocean
defining me from moment to moment.

The potential in life is not to use a knife on me
cutting out my femininity so badly.
I have nerve endings and pain receptors in my womb.

Someday I will find Jack to love me again
and take the pain away again.

They locked me up inside of me,
why is there injustice in life?

Sophia Jackson

Wilding conversations

It is here, in these conversations, that wilding becomes more tangible. It is 'the moment when I became myself' and 'wilding is power: connection to the life force, the universe; permission I give to myself'.

It is here, through these conversations, that this book starts to emerge in its present form, charting first the quest and wilding insight, then many women's many stories, and finally the themes and threads that weave through those stories. I write my story, then our collective story, then add everyone's stories, and finally the last section is explored collaboratively, as all of us read the stories and share our insights and thoughts and feelings.

In discussing this, we realise that the book – this book – is a handbook of support, a sharing of what has worked for individuals in the past and might well work for others now and in the future. As Arthur W Frank says about storytelling:

Storytelling is for an other just as much as it is for oneself. In the reciprocity that is storytelling, the teller offers herself as guide to the other's self-formulation. The other's receipt of that guidance not only recognises but values the teller. The moral genius of storytelling is that each, teller and listener, enters the space of the story for the other. Telling stories [...] attempts to change one's own life by affecting the lives of others.

Conversations are also starting about what wilding is for, what are we going to do with this knowledge, this energy? And as I was asked, what is the wilding call, the wilding path, how do we show up in the power of woman?

I have no idea how this will be done, happen, look like, or what it will be – but I absolutely trust the process.

And what a process. This is not about writing a book about wilding and putting it out into the world and hoping that women will read it and be influenced by it. Writing the book is just one part of how wilding spreads across the world person by person, act by act, story by story. Each woman who contributes a story takes a bit of wilding into her life from it, and talks to others, and acts in a wilding way on her wilding path. And people notice, and ask.

Who are these women?

We see how circles of friendship and connection intersect and overlap. The women who come together to write and share and read their stories come from links made through work and business, from academia, from school and student days, from dancing, from Parkinson's (this condition gives me extraordinary gifts, especially the gift of wonderful people), from the 1'59 project, from neighbours, from chance meetings, through art practice, through friends of friends – of friends – of friends.

The ripples from the pebbles of friendship thrown into the water spread out and out. Some of the women I have only met virtually and known for just a few months, others I have known for years, or decades. Some I am in close contact with, while others I see perhaps once every five or ten years.

There are gaps in the group, of women – dear friends – who have died. I like to think, to hope, that they too are contributing in some way.

We are the stories we tell ourselves about ourselves: words cast spells.

I am my own narrative. Each time I say 'I am this,' or 'I am that', then I am. The pathways in my brain and body that make things happen – that link intention and muscle – become stronger each time I travel them. Wilding is creating new paths for me, new desire lines of behaviour as I walk through the world.

Desire lines cut across the landscape, taking people from one place to another by intuitive routes, ignoring the formal paths laid out by architects or planners. In the same way wilding is cutting across my years of indoctrination, of meek acceptance of my place in the world.

The stories I tell myself about myself

The stories I have told myself about myself go way back into my childhood. As a young girl I haunted the local public library and, with any birthday money, I would set off for Thin's bookshop and spend a glorious morning trying to find the one book I would take home with me, the one I couldn't imagine living without. Sitting on the bookshop floor, leaning against the stacks, taking first one book, then another, putting them back, taking another, and doing it all over again until, mourning the books left behind, I took my choice to the till. I still have, and re-read, most of them. Rosemary Sutcliff's beautifully illustrated novels of Bronze Age and Roman Britain (*Warrior Scarlet; Dawn Wind; The Lantern Bearers; Outcast*) taught me about language, and the power of language and image combined.

They taught me about honesty and faithfulness and their cost. They taught me, too, that men are the actors in the world, and although women can be powerful it is only when compliant within a man's world – echoing the restrictions in Central Asian and Chinese myths. It has taken me many years, many decades, to unlearn this lesson. Of my many other childhood books, retained and re-read often, *The Phantom Tollbooth* taught me the joy of word play and puns; Edward Lear's nonsense poems showed me the power of rhythm and repetition. And through it all, steeped in story (reading below the bedclothes, hand poised to switch out the light when I heard my parents coming out of the living room) I absorbed the lesson of women's subordinate place in a man's world.

Even the songs we sang reinforced this: at school a favourite Scottish folk song was 'The Wee Cooper o' Fife'. The whole song is a justification of wife-beating, when a 'gentle' – that is, a gentlewoman – wife refuses to bake bread and brew beer for the household, and card and spin wool, because these activities are beneath her social status and might damage her fair skin and soft hands. The cooper puts a sheepskin on his wife's back and tells her that he will not beat *her*, but 'I will beat my ane (own) sheep skin'. The wife complies instantly. Extraordinary now to contemplate the society that could encourage teenage girls to celebrate domestic violence, rather than to recognise and condemn it.

You're back

STORY 27

It is a quarter to nine on a chilly damp November morning, and I am sitting on a bench in the park, my eighteen-month-old son asleep in his pushchair beside me. Neither my husband nor his live-in mistress can bear the sound of my son crying, so I have to take him out, whatever the weather, if he frets.

I hear someone saying my name, and look up to see a woman friend approaching and asking: Where have you been? I don't think I've seen you for at least two years – I heard you'd had a child, but this is the first time I've seen him. I start to tell her that I have been focusing on my life inside the family, balancing my receptionist work with looking after my child, and keeping house for my husband and our 'friend'. It all sounds perfectly normal to me.

The look on my friend's face is one of horror and disbelief – what am I saying? What do I mean, I have given up teaching that I love and am so good at? What is this 'friend' in the house? I try to tell her that we are all a loving family, that all is well, but it rings hollow. She changes the subject, we talk for a little longer, then she leaves. And I am left with the beginnings of questions.

The next day exactly the same thing happens. I am sitting on another bench in another park, early – it can't be later than half past eight – my child asleep in his pushchair, and another woman friend turns up. She asks the same questions as the previous friend – Where have you been? What's been happening in your life? What are these rumours and stories I've been hearing? I start to speak – and this time I speak about everything that has been happening, not trying to justify anything, or persuade myself or her that everything is fine. It is as if I am telling the story to myself for the first time, hearing it for the first time, hearing it with the same horror that I see in my friend's face, as in the previous day's friend's face.

In the eight long years of coercive control by my husband, he limited my career (I gave up a prestigious teaching role to become the receptionist in his osteopathic practice), forced his mistress (who in retrospect was as much a victim as I was) into our house and our bed, insisted she was there at the birth of our child, isolated me so thoroughly from my family that I never realised that my father was dying, and after his death abandoned my distraught mother.

Back in the park that second day, telling my story, the spell breaks. I go home completely clear. Disenchanted.

The next day is Monday. I phone an estate agent, get an estimate of what the house is worth, and make plans. After supper (I do all the cooking) I tell them I'm not doing this anymore, that she leaves, or I do. They don't believe me, and I find myself still in the situation a day later. So I pack a bag and take my child to stay with another girlfriend. Then my son and I get on a plane and fly to Scotland, and my mother.

She meets us off the plane, takes one long look at me and says: 'You're back.'

'Of course,' I say, 'I just got off the plane.'

'No,' she says. 'After all these years.

You're back.'

Quietly and insidiously the stories of my childhood told me that women are lesser creatures than men. Wilding is helping me to cut a path of my own across this distorted landscape.

In conversation we discover that while many of the women have had a similar experience of a compliant childhood, some have had rebellious childhoods fighting against the sense of being closed in, making their escape at the first possible moment. The conversations and stories hold all of this.

Each of our conversations has taken us deeper into wilding – what it means, what it is, how it shows up in our lives. And what it means in this community.

We talk, we share, we question, we put ideas forward, we build our thoughts and feelings collaboratively, creatively.

Trust

We build trust. At the start of the first conversation, we shared single words of how we were each feeling: interested/curious/emotional/nervous/anxious; and then again at the end: safe/inspired/very pleased to be invited/interested. We build a safe space where we can be free to feel and express emotion: 'What a charge I feel from our conversation and meeting! Thank you all for sharing, listening and holding space for everyone. I was so touched by the presence and genuine sharing. I felt like crying at times.'

We build a vision for the future of the book: 'This feels like it has been happening for a thousand years – this is the thread passed down by magical women, by magical agents' and 'This is a book that needs to be written now, for now.'

We start to build a sense of what wilding means to us as individuals, as women.

'Wilding is the moment when I became myself. When I became who I am.'

'The moment when I no longer am trying to be smaller than I am.'

Wilding is also how I sustain that moment, that momentum, that power. Through connection to the universe, to other women in this community, this tribe.

The permission I give myself to be myself.

It is also an acknowledgement that there is loss at the wilding point as well as gain; that change, that the wilding moment can happen at any age – in our seventies as well as when we are younger; and that it can happen once, or many times, over a lifetime.

Creating a wilding ecosystem

Living as a wilding woman in a society that is so often antagonistic to strong thoughtful women, can be hard. Being a wilding woman – having seen something in my life, my situation, myself, that changes everything – can be a lonely place. As one of the wilding women, says:

Very few people understand my evolution. The others say, you have changed, we don't recognise you. What is happening? Are you ill? This is the price to pay for me, to have become a wilding woman. And I regret nothing.

The metaphor of a biological ecosystem is a useful framework to consider the part society plays in supporting, or not, wilding women, and the value placed on wilding thought and action. Wilding in the wider society is itself an output of a human ecosystem, as well as of individuals. In creating a wilding women community, we are creating a supportive ecosystem. Any organism – human or otherwise – needs its biological ecosystem to survive. Making a radical shift into changing a way of life needs not just that moment of seeing, the wilding moment, but a social environment, a community that supports those changes. The wilding woman goes on to say:

New friends, new life, and I have never been so happy to be a wilding woman.

We are exploring what the properties of an ecosystem – the social, emotional, spiritual, as well as physical environment – that would sustain wilding, sustain us living as wilding women might be.

Courage

Becoming, *being* a wilding woman needs courage: a wilding ecosystem provides en-courage-ment. In our regular conversations we explore how we have reacted to challenges, what their impact has been, and how we have learned from them. We point out other women's successes that they might have been too close to, to see and appreciate. Wilding women are curious and explore their world: a wilding ecosystem creates the opportunity to play with ideas, to discuss, question and challenge assumptions. Women make new friends, create new contacts. Wilding is not just something an individual woman experiences, it is also the wider social context each of us finds ourselves in. The question becomes: How might we create a wilding ecosystem that works for each of us, and all of us, and women everywhere? If different bits of a wilding women ecology are missing, how can we identify them and put them in place?

Community

In our conversations we talk about this:

'We are building a community.'

'The word community was mentioned – this is how it feels to me. We are building a community within a community within a community, a lineage of thousands of years of strong women! Another one of you spoke about the timeliness of this. So true!! I am really excited to be a part of this community. I am honoured.'

And:

'It's so important that we stand together, holding hands. We are good at it, us women.'

We are building a community – Sarah M. used the word tribe – not a group. We are not 'joiners', not people to subsume ourselves within a group; instead we are powerful women bringing our growing power and skills to change ourselves, our communities and our worlds.

We are building a reflective practice: 'I'd better get writing. I had a fairly clear idea that I'd write about a turning point that had felt 100% positive to me. But during the meeting, I realised that it did come at a cost, and so I feel now that I might write two shorter pieces reflecting that... fascinating that meeting you all has already influenced me.'

We are building new ways of seeing and of being: 'fearless,' Carrie said. Soo Young said that our conversations reminded her that true inner freedom comes with loss. Only with a cleared space can the fresh breeze blow through.

We are building life:

'This is such an interesting adventure and I'm so looking forward to contributing and sharing our stories.'

And it is a continuous beginning; a continuous ending; a continuous seeking, finding, letting go, discovering, mistaking, reflecting, failing, making.

Living, in other words – living.

And then the stories start to arrive...

CHAPTER FOURTEEN

Wilding stories

'I like living. I have sometimes been wildly, despairingly, acutely miserable, racked with sorrow, but through it all I still know quite certainly that just to be alive is a grand thing.' Agatha Christie

'My thriving is dependent on an intentional seclusion to find meaning in the wondrous encounters in my life.' Soo Young Lee

Meeting the wilding women

Reading and re-reading the stories is a continual joy – every time I do, I see something new about the narrative, about the writer, and about me. Things I have missed first time round, the nuances, the links, the choices, changes and challenges, stand out more clearly. The subtleties of expression and emotions are very moving. I am in awe of the writers' courage and vulnerability, their openness, their humour and the power of their storytelling.

Where else would I meet women who open themselves to life with such generosity, holding and nurturing their children, their parents, their grandparents regardless of their own circumstances, while at the same time learning to hold and nurture themselves? Women who seek and create warm spaces for living and thriving for themselves and their families; women who swim in lakes with Oxum, the Afro-Brazilian river goddess; women who describe themselves 'as an edge-stalker, I want to swim in the air and walk in the water'; who see their life as a dam holding back a great weight of emotional water that sweeps over them when the dam finally gives way, washing away the old abusive life and leaving the way clear for new and loving possibilities.

Women who come to terms with their sexuality, joyfully and proudly; women who take a deep breath when faced with illness and unforeseen life changes and look for the gifts each experience brings; women who find their spiritual selves, who birth their spiritual selves into being, with joy and pain and elation; women who delight in discovering the wonders of the natural world and the marvels of their own interior worlds.

Women who explore the power of myth and legend, and folk tales, connecting with ancient goddesses, creating their own avatars, rewriting, recreating their stories, their life narrative.

As I read, I hear echoes of my own journey and remember learning I had forgotten or avoided. I recall moments of facing down my fears, of finding strength and courage through laughter. Words that protected me or opened me up to a new perspective, a fresh way of looking at things and – above all – the sudden clarity, the split second of insight that shone a light on a sorcerer's spell and freed me from it.

Free from the enchantment

Funny – or perhaps unsurprising – that the word 'disenchantment' carries a freight of disappointment, of sadness and, sometimes, cynicism. Whereas for me and many of the story-writers, disenchantment is a moment of joy, of exhilaration, when the enchantment breaks and the truth, the true nature of the enchantment, shows up in all its glory and discomfort, and I can get on with life.

So many of the stories are about the writer recognising she is trapped within a bubble, a pattern, of someone else's making – made by society and its expectations, by a controlling other person – and then breaking out of it, fracturing the pattern and becoming fully herself. Breaking a bubble, breaking a life pattern, is hard work, and many of the stories are about this: stories of women being stuck in what they see as their obligations to a parent or spouse, then slowly – or indeed suddenly – seeing their situation for what it is: exploitative and abusive and stepping out of the trap. Some of the stories touch on the difficulties the writers faced after stepping out of the bubble – friends and partners who found the change too much for them to handle and wanted the writer to go back to their previous predictable state.

It might be tempting to read victimhood into the stories, but that would be to read them through a distorting lens. These are stories filled with joy – a word I unashamedly keep coming back to – and joy on so many different levels. The joys of friendship and laughter; the huge joys of falling in love, of rediscovering a deep love and appreciation of a parent; the small quotidian joys of swimming after a hard day's labouring, or catching sight of a bird, or sheep grazing on a hillside; the quiet joys of the woods, the seashore, the hills and fields.

The stories face the big issues of life and of birth; of life and illness and death. The stories cross the generations as the writers explore their own childhoods and those of their children, their relationships with their parents and their parental relationship with their own children, the important place of grandparents in their lives. There are stories of women grasping the fact of their illness with both hands and moving through and beyond it – skydiving, dancing, striking out for a new and renewed life. Looking for the gifts in their new state.

Gratitude

Gratitude resonates through the stories, gratitude for life itself and all the joys life brings; gratitude for the ability to see and appreciate life's gifts;

gratitude for the continuous learning and growing and becoming oneself fully and deeply.

A strong thread of spirituality weaves through the stories. Spirituality in many different aspects: as a strong belief in a religious god, as connecting with the pantheistic spirits of nature, as exploring and celebrating the mysteries of ancient goddesses and myths. Spirituality as a deep understanding of our own spirit, our internal life, our connections between inner and outer worlds, between perception (looking outward) and interoception (looking inward).

Interwoven with the spiritual there is a thread of the body: spirit as the weft and body as the warp, together weaving the whole cloth of the storytellers' humanity. Body in sickness and in health, body exploited, body celebrated, discovered and explored. Body living and dying.

The stories have one thing in common – the conviction, the deep knowledge, that the story is worth the telling. The days are, in the main, gone when 'women's literature' was dismissed as trivial and of no or little account, when to be great literature the writing had to be about manly stuff like blood and guts and death (as if women do not have a far more intimate acquaintance with blood and guts and death than many men).

Virginia Woolf, in the 1920s and '30s talks about 'women's as yet unnarrated lives', about 'the accumulation of unrecorded life' piled up from 'all these infinitely obscure lives' that remain to be recorded. There is a palpable joy as the writers write and send their stories, a real hunger to be heard, a glorious light shining through the words, illuminating the unrecorded lives, narrating the obscure, voicing previously unvoiced hidden thoughts and feelings. The story writing has made these experiences real, given them the worth they deserve, not only to the writers, but also the readers.

The process of writing our stories has caused us to dig deep into ourselves. It is not easy, to uncover things that have been buried for shame, or for fear. It is not easy to write about the joy (that word again!) that springs in the heart, or the warmth that floods the body and mind, when someone or something arrives. And it is not easy to go deep and deeper into each experience until the core, the essence, is there. So simple, so clear, so joyful.

An invitation: Gratitude

When my husband died, I was distraught. I would wake up very
early and not know what to do with myself. Then I heard him
very clearly saying (as he used to) 'And your problem is...?' I took
myself out of the house to the nearest park and as I walked, I
made a gratitude list in my head. What do I have to be grateful
for that starts with the letter A? Then B; then C; until I had gone
all the way to Z. By then I was able to face the day.

Make a gratitude list for yourself...

Living and Dying in the Game

There are games for the body, games for the mind, but what about games for the soul? Today, most people think of computer games as just another form of entertainment; a diversion from their daily lives' mundane nature. I worked in the computer game industry and often thought of games that way; until I experienced the transformational power of games.

I played a game called World of Warcraft, a multiplayer fantasy game; as you progress through the game, you are faced with quests necessary for your avatar to level up. Often when you failed a quest, you died. Now for the longest time, I did not play games where my character died. I don't think it was intentional. It was just that the types of games I chose to play didn't involve death. I found that when I did play such games, I was horrified. I was sickened.

In reality, when you die in a game, most view this game mechanic as a representation of your ultimate failure in the game. You do something wrong, Pac-Man dies, or Mario falls down the cliff. But they don't really. You just start again. You learn from your mistakes. Isn't that what we all do when we fail?

The character I played in WoW was a shaman troll named Tahara. I knew that if I wanted to level her up to become a shaman, she would have to die in the game. But I was torn.

I began to think it wasn't fair to keep her at low levels because of my fear of death. Was I keeping her fearful of evolving? Of growing up? Was I the one fearful of death? Her death. My death. Our death.

It was during this time that I was diagnosed with cancer. While intellectually, I knew that my prognosis was good, I didn't want to experience death—real or virtual. When I would log on to the game and begin playing, I would look for the lower-level quests. The ones in which we were less likely to die. My friends thought I was ridiculous.

Maybe that was true. But I was terrified of seeing Tahara die in front of me. I knew there wouldn't be blood. It would be a silent death. I knew that this was just the 'failure as quest game mechanic'. So why was I scared? Why did it matter what it might feel like? What if that ghostly figure which appeared after you died was the physical me looking up at the angel of death? What would death feel like in a video game if it was me in the game? These questions plagued me while I struggled with my thoughts on my life, death, and mortality.

Sometimes while playing, I jumped back from my keyboard. My fingers shaking as the enemies surrounded me. I would start shooting my spells but often to no avail.

As an interim step to help me deal with these fears, I started by playing in a third-person view, sometimes called 'god view'. From this perspective, I was the watcher, even if it was me I was watching. As I grew more confident, I began trying to play in first person. From looking at the robbers from a distance and seeing Tahara on the screen fighting them, I was now Tahara looking directly into their faces and fighting them at close range. Did I die? Of course. Many times. I was playing in the moment. I told myself that it was just a video game. That is was not a prediction of my future.

Instead of worrying about

death, my character's failure to achieve what the game thought was necessary to succeed... to win... perhaps, there was another approach to the game. Living.

Instead of fearing death, I started to take risks in the game. Instead of hiding behind rocks or waiting until the thieves had left, I/we took a bolder approach. We entered the battle zone; we quested with others. I watched Tahara level up and grow. I began to experience and celebrate her virtual life rather than live in fear of death. Through her, I became bolder, more assertive in the risks I was willing to take. Yes, we did die in the game. But we learned to resurrect ourselves and learn from our actions.

We learned not only how to die but also how to live.

CHAPTER FIFTEEN

Wilding Women's voices

'The stories are beads on a necklace of power.'

The last word goes to the wilding women, as they speak for themselves in conversations and email, discussing the stories, drawing out their shared insights, exploring the threads and themes running through them. They talk about how they wrote their story, and the inner learning and emotions that accompanied the process. They share the impact of reading others' stories.

Writing our stories

It was profoundly liberating writing our stories: 'I've never written about this before' 'Thank you for giving us the chance to tell our stories'. We found it challenging, cathartic, difficult. It took a while for some of us to decide what to write about, what to include – and at the other extreme, we could be quite impulsive. Sometimes we condensed different memories.

Then we had to decide on how to tell the story – in prose or poetry. Some of the stories 'wrote themselves' – others took many days or even weeks of wrestling with ideas, with form, with content. We identified different writing approaches; some were straightforward reflective narratives, others an examination of the sacred feminine, and some a combination of the two, and more.

The process behind the stories – how we wrote them – turns out to be every bit as important as the content – what we wrote. The process is what makes the stories so powerful: reflecting on our lives, choosing, then writing about a particular experience, sharing our story and reading other women's stories. The process is what makes the stories so readily accessible to other women, other stories. Storytelling, as Frank said, is both for the listener and for the teller – each learns and grows through the process.

Writing rather than speaking the stories allowed us to go deeply into the feelings, into the lived experience, in our own time, in our own ways. It was, for many of us, less difficult than telling the story out loud to another person – which risked feeling more like therapy, or confession. Writing also gave us the chance to recognise all-too-familiar patterns of blame and guilt, and to challenge and rethink, reframe, those patterns. The physical act of writing – whether with pen on paper or typing it out – somehow freed up our memories and pulled details out that had lain forgotten, or suppressed, for many years.

Reading our stories

We sent the stories, anonymised, to everyone in the group, to read them all and then share our responses with each other. We saw how beautiful the stories were – honest, open, inspiring, very rich. We saw how they chronicled small liberations as well as life-changing ones, how they celebrated baby steps as well as great strides. We admired our shared capacity for resilience.

The process was such a strong one: reflect, write, share, read, reflect, write more, share again, read more – and we found we kept coming back to the beginning, to the reflection.

We felt that in reading the stories we gained insight into our own lives as well as into the writer's. We realised that however huge the issues we were reading about, we could be more relaxed about similar issues in our own lives – after all, the writer had not only survived what she had been going through, but had come out the other side stronger, happier, and more powerful. If she could, we reckoned, then we could. Back to Brené Brown's 'survival guide'.

Reading the stories helped us connect with ourselves, with how we are, with where we are going – our own desire lines, our wilding path. It helped us to become aware of women's sensibility, the way individual women think. Reading the stories underpinned our own transitions from our pre-wilding state to our wilding selves.

Reading the stories, we felt amazement, great pride in being a woman, proud of other women, an acute awareness of the writers' vulnerability ('I'm naked, and I'm okay') and trust. We felt gratitude at being included and a conviction that: 'This is the only place where our stories can be told...' '...and heard'.

Trust

We were intrigued by the level of trust generated in the group that enabled the stories to be safely shared and the conversations to happen. For many of us this was the first time we had spoken out about our experiences; we relished the beauty of having the opportunity, to trust the situation enough to tell very personal stories. As Shelley said, echoing the Jung quote above:

'Sometimes our story harbours shame, so we keep it inside. By telling the story, we liberate ourselves of the secret. This can have a big positive impact on our lives.'

We have a need to speak our true selves, and there are obstacles to doing that. We spent time exploring the conditions that allow us to speak up; what is it that creates the trust?

If the trust works in this group, how do we protect it? We have a need to speak our true selves, but there are obstacles in the way. What are the conditions that allow us to speak up – what is okay in the group, in the book, on the website?

And we concluded that clear, light-touch boundaries and protocols are an essential part of holding safe, trusting, and challenging conversations. We clarified these as a set of simple guidelines:

All the voices are heard – there is space for everyone to speak.

All the voices are heard – no one is obliged to speak.

All the voices are heard – uninterrupted, not cut across.

All the voices are heard – each takes responsibility for her own time-taking and turn-taking.

As a result, each of us is able to say:

I feel included, valued and respected as I am.

I feel empowered to bring my full agency, to be the author of my own life.

I feel nourished, sharing from my own experience and truth – I speak only for myself, not for others.

I feel safe to say my truth, knowing that what I say will be heard with respect and appreciation by everyone, whether or not they agree with me.

Impact and purpose

What is the purpose of writing and sharing the stories? Is there a purpose?

There is a craving to have our voices heard; there is gratitude to our younger selves, for our resilience, strength and youth – honouring ourselves and our sense of continuity.

We wondered – will younger women have a different experience – is the experience different for them? We wondered – what is universal about it all?

We answered: Moving from one state to another, from uncertainty to understanding; from fear to illumination; from prejudice to joy (and occasionally shock); from breakdown of our own judgement to clarity.

We found that reading the stories 'motivated me to pay more attention to me'. That it 'helped me to get clarity about my life, seeing what needs to happen, and to stop wavering'. Above all, reading the stories gave me permission to be ME, to find my expanded identity, my true voice.

We saw that all the stories are connected – beads in the necklace. Each one is a woman's story and it's bigger than just one story. The stories are all the women's stories; for some writers anonymity gives power. For others, the power comes from claiming our story.

Threads and themes

We found themes running through the stories, common threads of growth and change:

'The thing that has moved through me is the sense of a powerful rediscovery of Self in the women's stories.'

'We are all the same. We are not alone. We are all extremely creative and powerful. We have the ability to heal and find peace in the chaos we are born into.'

Resurrection from despair, loss and being lost.

Rejuvenation of dreams, self and spirit.

Reclamation of healing, empowerment and love.

Our bodies: Birth, death and illness

Throughout the stories there are many references to our bodies, to their wonderful and their difficult aspects. There are stories of illnesses – our own and others' – and how we have found meaning in illness. For example, finding a meaning in a Parkinson's diagnosis, a meaning in the condition. In one story this is slowing down and enjoying things that in a busy previous life there was no time for. In another to help others with the same condition.

Then there are references, almost in passing, of the joy of bodies – of swimming in a wild river, of holding our children and of giving birth to them.

Death of loved ones is, for many of us, our wilding moment when we reassess our lives and what we want from life for ourselves and for those we love.

There are also themes of the psychic body – of psychic death and rebirth of self and spirit, of multiple rebirthings, and of the healing that happens in our bodies and our souls.

And through it all, the strong theme of finding meaning, finding healing, finding joy in illness and death, physical and psychic.

Being a woman in the world

The very starting point of wilding made it inevitable that so many of the stories would examine what we called 'getting beyond the corset' the metaphor of the corset that our grandmothers and great-grandmothers had to wear to conform to contemporary ideas of womanhood and beauty, the ideas that required constriction, required women to keep their place, lesser in the eyes of society and the law. There is a theme through the stories of bursting out, of unlacing ourselves, of rebelling, transforming. We talk about shedding a skin; emerging from a chrysalis as a butterfly; no longer 'tame'; moving beyond stereotypes.

And at the heart of this theme, the realisation of our own personal and growing power – to be ourselves, to find peace and stability, to take back control, and to embrace adventure. To (re)discover the raw, animal, divine, connected, powerful woman-self: selfhood.

Resilience, freedom and joy

There is, we discovered, a strong theme of courage and fortitude, of grit and determination, of resilience. Discovering what it takes to be, and continue to be, powerfully Me, powerfully understanding myself.

And along with the resilience goes the theme of freedom and joy, when we are alive to the possibility of ourselves. There is, we found, a theme of how we have moved from victim to surviving to thriving to shining and beauty. There is a thread of healing and awakening, a theme of being the brave curious child; a theme of opening out to beautiful breaking, opening, and unravelling.

In story after story, we learn how the writer has recovered the bold child who had been tamed and conditioned by parents and society to be the 'good daughter' the 'good wife' the 'good mother'. We shared the difficulties and strength needed to overcome them – sometimes having to leave an over-dependent mother or over-possessive partner.

We discover and use the power of nature – uncultivated, feral, wild, free, whole; the power of the elements and elemental forces.

We talk of the joy of escaping alone in nature to discover or rediscover our genuine self; the life path, the wilding path, the desire line, that is entirely our own choice. We explore being open to whatever the experience of aloneness sends to us, even if it is scary.

And we relish the fun that we experience through our freedom, and the joy it brings.

How do we do this?

There is a thread winding through the stories – explicitly or implicitly below the surface – of how we have each managed to do this – to find ourselves in our wilding moment, to recognise it and change our life.

We do this through letting go, through grieving, through keening. Keening is the sound we make when we are grieving – the letting go, loss and grief, leaving behind and making space for the new – rising like a phoenix from ashes of our old life.

Appreciating the rewards – that the grief is worth it.

We do this through inner work – through intuition and hard work; a deep-dive spiral that moves down to do the inner work, then up to resurrect ourselves. We do this by becoming aware of the cycles of our lives – leading deeper into the process of ourselves. We recognise, yet again, the patterns of behaviour that hinder us from being fully and joyfully ourselves, and we start to deconstruct the old patterns and build new shining ones.

Minna Salami's quotation bears repeating here: 'There are realizations from which you can never return, light-bulb moments that shape your destiny by revealing the constellations of your behaviour.'

Meta-themes

Johanna identified other threads and themes that are common across the stories:

Environment – rural and urban; house and home; foreign countries and home; inner and outer; micro and macro; night and day; unknown and known; public transport; nurture and nature

Nature – birds; water; trees; desert; sky

Relationships – with nature; parents; spouse/partner; children; God; body, mind, soul; one's Self; sex; opposite gender; same gender; spirituality

The Body – disease; prison; disabled; vessel; mannequin; shell; puberty; sex; legs; hips; breasts; cancer; Parkinson's

Emotions – fear; anger; despair; hurt; passivity; content; relief; elated; peaceful; sadness; loss; triumph; achievement; awkward; anxiety; panic; gratitude; frustration

Physiology – heartache; cold; breathing

Actions – letting go; positive and negative; change of environment; moving from one location to another; stillness; self-exploration (therapy, workshops, education, counselling)

Liberation – leaving spouse/partner; doing one's heart's desires; being in a safe environment; being with the people who matter

Symbols – a cardinal bird; a house; a tattoo; a tree

And finally, Carol wrote:

I am impressed by the generosity of spirit which all the wilding women have shown in sharing their memories, thoughts, vision and giving us windows into their lives.

In some of the contributions there is pain; in others, joy; in almost all there is a searching for meaning – the core of what being a woman means. Some of us already have a clear idea of what we are about. Our feet are firmly grounded and our eyes look forward with confidence. Others are more tentative and are searching for an ideal. Will this ever, in reality, ever be fully realised?

We are on a journey through life where some paths lead straight and true, and others meander. Sometimes we take a path leading to a dead end and need to retrace our steps to gain a better perspective.

From sharing these pieces of introspection with each other, perhaps we will now look outward, moving into exploration of the contribution which, collectively as well as individually, we can/do make to society in general and to those around us. Like dropping a pebble into a pool, I see the contributions we have all made as part of a process, with the ripples flowing outward in concentric circles.

We wished each other a 'Hopeful New Year'!

A woman's liberation on Freedom and Democracy Day in Prague

STORY 29

A woman rushes to catch a tram
past two students in conversation
while putting a loaf of bread in her
bag.

A woman and a man have coffee
on a bench as a woman
walks an unleashed bitch.

A woman and a child
eat ice cream spying on
a man stepping onto the bridge.

A woman paddles
under clouds
in a city rowboat
as a swan slowly passes
with her chicks.

A woman performs
a scene at a desk
with a typewriter
in the middle of a square.

A woman crosses the river
on a tightrope
while a crowd watches
on television.

A woman sings
A Prayer for Marta
on the balcony
of the National Theater
on November 17th.

Index of story themes

*In the wilding stories, each writer bears witness
to her own reality, describing her wilding
moment, when the unacceptable circumstances
of her life, invisible for so long, become visible
and nothing is ever the same again.*

The wilding process

In writing her story, each writer is 'bearing witness to reality', as Rebecca
Solnit puts it. The reality's unacceptability is no longer glossed over but
seen for what it is: something unacceptable that has been buried, gaslit,
obfuscated and distorted. And in making its unacceptability visible, each
writer uses her voice, as Solnit says, 'to open up space for other voices'.

The stories describe their authors' wilding process: a build-up of
dissatisfaction and discomfort – being fed up being fed up; then a wilding
moment of clarity; followed by reflection and acceptance of what they have
seen so clearly. The wilding women talk about how they then reimagine
their life, see the changes they want to make, make them (and deal with
other people's often hostile responses to their changes), and maintain the
changes, continuing to learn, to grow, to get stronger, to become ever more
powerfully wilding. 'I don't have to make myself small anymore.'

Build-up of
dissatisfaction
and discomfort

Wilding
moment of
clarity

Reflection
and
acceptance

Reframing
and
reimagining
life

Making
changes:
discovery &
learning

Resources for
growing the
changes

At each step of the process (and it's rarely as straightforward as this) we find we are dealing with different strong emotions, different challenges. There will be someone's story, some set of circumstances, that resonates with where you are right now – use this index to guide you towards the woman's experience that can give you the strength and hope you need to get through where you are at the moment, and out the other side.

THE WILDING PROCESS

Joyeux Noel

Ma vie trainait... en couple sans vraiment l'être, mon enfant élevé en commun formait un triangle de liens malgré nos discordes. Depuis 9 années, on vivait sous le même toit, de plus en plus étrangers. La rupture devait arriver, peut-être, ou sûrement. Je venais d'acheter une maison pour être indépendante sans forcément nous séparer. Je voulais tester notre relation hors de ce quotidien qui nous minaient. La rupture est arrivée pendant les travaux, un 23 décembre. J'étais en voiture avec mon fils pour aller passer noël dans ma famille, mon téléphone a sonné. Arrêtée au bord de la route, j'ai écouté mon conjoint crier qu'il était en train de jeter toutes mes affaires par la fenêtre, dans des sacs poubelles, sur l'herbe, sous la pluie. La jalousie et l'alcool justifiaient son attitude : j'étais coupable, il se vengeait. Que faire ? Demi-tour et mettre mon fils au cœur de cette tempête ? J'ai appelé des amis sur place, leur ai demandé de prendre la clé de la grange des voisins dans l'entrée de notre maison, de tout ramasser et l'entasser là-bas.

Quelques jours plus tard, il m'a dit « tu vois ce que tu me fais faire », j'ai grimacé au bout du fil... Il n'était plus en colère mais triste et inquiet de ce qu'il adviendrait de lui vis-à-vis de mon fils de 10 ans. Sur ce point j'étais très claire : leur relation n'avait pas à souffrir de la nôtre. Je ferai tout pour qu'elle perdure s'il s'en sentait l'envie. Il continuerait donc de le garder le lundi soir, car depuis le 14 décembre, je venais de trouver un travail de 3 jours par semaine à 70 kms.

Partie pour 2 semaines, je suis rentrée plus tôt, sans mon fils, pour chercher un logement, une chambre, un gîte, bref un refuge pour mon fils et moi. Je suis aussi passée voir l'étendue des dégâts parmi mes affaires entassées dans la grange : des livres abîmés, des vêtements collés tâchés d'encre de Chine, des bijoux perdus... « Que du matériel » ai-je pensé ! J'étais étrangement sereine, juste préoccupée d'organiser la vie à venir. Une amie m'a offert une grande chambre avec 3 lits dans son grenier ou j'ai installé un nid accueillant avec quelques cartons pour y mettre vêtements, livres et jouets. Nous avons campé 8 mois dans cette vie entre-deux.

Durant cette période, aidée d'un maçon, j'ai avancé les travaux comme un forçat, 4 jours par semaine, 12h par jour, le corps parfois en souffrance mais l'esprit libre ! Pendant le rush final de l'été, un étang m'a sauvée ! Après les journées de chantier, j'allais nager, remercier Oxum en chantant, délasser mes muscles dans la puissance de l'eau et finir par une salutation au soleil couchant ! Le 31 août, veille de la rentrée scolaire, nous habitions enfin notre maison !

Quand ma vie a basculé

J'avais 28 ans, j'étais enceinte de 6 mois. Un coup de fil m'apprend un jour que ma grand-mère a un cancer. Je me rappelle encore le tremblement qui a traversé mon ventre déjà bien rond, comme un signal vers un avenir empli d'incertitudes. Autant que possible, j'accompagne ma grand-mère contrainte à de nombreuses séances de chimiothérapie. Elle prend le train chaque semaine pour se rendre à l'hôpital et repartir chez elle le lendemain. Elle s'épuise mais elle tient à son autonomie. Semaine après semaine, ses cheveux tombent, sa peau blémit et se flétrit, elle en perd sa bonne humeur et sa joie de vivre. Je suis partagée entre un immense bonheur d'accueillir bientôt mon premier enfant et une infinie tristesse de voir ma grand-mère s'éteindre doucement.

Naissance de mon fils, joie immense, bonheur de la maternité. Après de longs mois de souffrance, son traitement est interrompu car il ne réussira pas à la guérir, les métastases se diffusent partout.

Dans le même temps, contrainte à cette proximité soudaine et envahissante avec la maladie, j'apprends que je suis également atteinte d'un cancer, la thyroïde. Un cancer sympa me dit le chirurgien ! Jour après jour, je m'occupe de mon fils, je continue de vivre mais j'ai l'impression que mes jours sont comptés. Alors que je n'avais aucun symptôme, je me sens comme trahie par mon corps, et le sentiment permanent que ma vie m'échappe inéluctablement, que je vais certainement mourir. Au réveil de l'opération, je découvre la chambre que je partage avec deux autres personnes, j'entends les voix des infirmières, les bruits des chariots qui crissent sur le sol, et je m'étonne d'être encore là, vivante. Encore un mois de traitement et les médecins m'annoncent que je suis sortie d'affaire.

Je reprends doucement pieds avec la vie, je retrouve le contact quelque peu perdu avec mon fils, qui doit se demander dans quel triste monde il est arrivé. Ma grand-mère est prise en charge dans un centre de soins paliatifs et les visites que je lui rends m'anéantissent chaque fois un peu plus. Elle me dit un jour, « une vie arrive, une autre s'en va » mais je ne veux pas accepter qu'elle partira bientôt.

Lors des visites suivantes, elle ne se lève plus, puis ne parle plus, puis ne voit plus, puis plus rien. Elle semblait dormir, dans une sorte de coma pré-mortem. Je renonçais à ces visites, trop douloureuses. Le jour où je reprenais un nouveau travail, j'apprenais qu'elle était morte, dans la nuit. Je décide malgré tout que le désespoir n'aura pas le dessus et que je m'en sortirai pour lui, mon fils, pour lui (dé)montrer que la vie peut aussi être joyeuse, heureuse, légère. Le souvenir de cette période si intense en émotions opposées reste un moment de bascule violent entre mon statut de jeune femme, fille et petite-fille, et celui de jeune mère. Cette épreuve m'a néanmoins appris à m'extasier de chaque nouvelle journée qui commence, de chaque petit bonheur qui m'est offert, de chaque rencontre et du plaisir qu'il y a à vivre tout simplement.

Quand ma vie a basculé 2

Rétrospectivement, je me suis représentée ma vie tenue par un immense barrage. Avec le temps, l'eau qui s'était artificiellement accumulée en amont pesait si lourdement que des fissures étaient apparues. Jour après jour, des petits morceaux de pierre se détachaient et roulaient au sol, l'eau commençait à s'exfiltrer, à vouloir s'échapper. Il m'aborda un jour dans la rue, un orage éclata. Echange de numéros, on se revit quelques jours plus tard dans un café. Ses yeux bleus souriants, ses grandes mains, sa voix douce et hésitante m'assurèrent de sa bienveillance. Je m'autorisais à tomber amoureuse et le barrage céda, explosa littéralement. L'eau contenue si longtemps se déversa en torrents m'offrant un immense sentiment de légèreté et un bonheur aussi puissant qu'inattendu.

Dans ma vie d'avant, j'avais tellement intégré l'opposition, la violence verbale, le silence que je ne pouvais pas envisager qu'un autre modèle existe. En apparence, nous formions une famille heureuse et unie, c'est vrai, mais au fond de moi, les gouttes d'eau s'accumulaient, j'avalais les reproches, le mépris et le fiel sans pouvoir modifier le rapport établi. Je sentais bien que ça ne « collait » plus mais je ne parvenais pas à le penser avec des mots et encore moins à imaginer qu'une autre vie était possible. Après coup, je me suis rendue compte à quel point je me sentais isolée, oppressée - j'avais du mal à respirer parfois sans faire le rapprochement -, entre mes charges familiales et professionnelles, satisfaisantes à bien des endroits certes, mais ancrées dans un emploi du temps minuté et sans espace de pensée ni de respiration, aucun.

Epuisée aussi de devoir affronter tant d'adversité pour faire valoir mon identité, faire entendre ma voix et mes désirs, qui lui paraissait le plus souvent déplacés, naïfs, inconscients, voire même inutiles : « A quoi bon te fatiguer à faire du pain puisqu'il y a une boulangerie au coin de la rue ? ».

Epuisée encore de tirer cette charge trop lourde pour moi, cette force contraire, qui trop souvent m'empêchait d'avancer. Je n'ai pu m'extirper que brutalement de cet homme possessif et jaloux qui ne cesse, aujourd'hui encore, après cinq ans de séparation, de m'agresser verbalement, mais je tiens bon.

J'apprends depuis ce que c'est que de vivre libre, et c'est comme une renaissance. En quittant mes habitudes, mon conditionnement et mes anciennes convictions, mes attaches et mes liens, j'accepte tous les possibles pour me (re)trouver : « avoir toujours été celle que je suis et être si différente de celle que j'étais » (Samuel Becket, O les beaux jours, 1963). J'ai trouvé l'espace de donner libre cours à ma créativité, de prendre du plaisir, sous le regard d'un homme aimant et drôle. Je ris aussi, et c'est la meilleure des thérapies !

Wilding women references

Reading has always been a joy for me – becoming immersed in another world, in someone else's thinking. Reading takes me into Kairos time yet again, and I swim in the ideas and images that the books open up. Writing this book has taken me back into my childhood reading, it has given me a new perspective on reading I did for my academic work, and has opened up my curiosity when coming across books and topics and authors serendipitously. My neighbour across the road reads voraciously, and lends me feminist thrillers. A friend recommends Dickens, an author I managed with some skill (and pride) to avoid reading at school, then I pick up The Old Curiosity Shop from the shelf in a hotel lounge and find myself absorbed. On my bookshelves Margaret Atwood rubs shoulders with Montaigne, Fay Weldon with Virginia Woolf, and Jane Austen with Roxanne Gay.

Here are the books, the writers, the activists and thinkers mentioned in the previous chapters who have enriched this book – I hope that you will find them thought-provoking and absorbing, and will share others of your own. They are grouped loosely by theme.

Feminist/political

Mary Wollstonecraft: *A Vindication of the Rights of Woman: With Strictures on Political and Moral Subjects* (1792). (One of the earliest works of feminist philosophy, a response to those educational and political theorists of the 18th century who did not believe women should receive a rational education.)

Emmeline Pankhurst 1858 – 1928   (Best remembered for organising the UK suffragette movement and helping women win the right to vote.)

Shirley Chisholm 1924 – 2005 (The first African American woman to have a seat in Congress and the first woman and African American woman to seek a Democratic Party nomination for President of the United States.)

Betty Freidan: *The Feminine Mystique* (1963)

Audre Lorde: *Sister Outsider: Essays and Speeches* (1984). (Self-described "black, lesbian, mother, warrior, poet.")

bell hooks: *Feminist Theory from Margin to Centre* (1984)

Roxanne Gay: *Bad Feminist*

Rebecca Solnit: Men explain things to me; Recollections of my non-existence (and many more)

Wilding women in history, legend and myth

Clarissa Pinkola Estès: *Women who run with the wolves: Myths and stories of the wild woman archetype.*

Barbara G Walker: *The Woman's Encyclopedia of Myths and* Secrets; *The Crone: Women of Age, Wisdom and Power*

Wilding in nature and indigenous wisdom

Isabella Tree: *Wilding: The Return of Nature to a British Farm*

George Monbiot: *Feral*

Richard Mabey: *Food for free*

Simon Barnes: *Rewild Yourself: 23 Spellbinding Ways to Make Nature More Visible*

Suzanne Simard: *Finding the Mother Tree: Uncovering the Wisdom and Intelligence of the Forest*

Robin Wall Kimmerer: *Braiding Sweetgrass; Gathering Moss*

Wilding in literature, poetry, philosophy and art

Christopher Alexander: *A Pattern Language*

Margaret Boden: *The Creative Mind*

Rupert Brooks: *The Great Lover (In: Poetry anthologies)*

Walter de la Mare: *Silver*

Arthur W. Frank: *The Wounded Storyteller*

Sara Houston: *Feeling Lovely*

Clare Hunter: *Threads of Life: A History of the World Through the Eye of a Needle*

Norton Juster: *The Phantom Tolbooth*

John Montague *Hymns to the Silence (In: 'The Hill of Silence')*

Alice Munro: *Dear Life*

Mary Oliver: *When I am among the trees (In: Devotions: Selected poetry)*

Alastair Reid: *Scotland (In: Inside Out – Selected Poetry and Translations)*

Minna Salami: *Sensuous Knowledge: A black feminist approach for everyone*

Rosemary Sutcliffe: *Warrior Scarlet; Dawn Wind; The Lantern Bearers; Outcast*

Jill L Vincent: *The Mathematics of Sundials*

Oscar Wilde: *The Selfish Giant*

Virginia Woolf: *Professions for Women; A Room of One's Own*

Internet links:

Brené Brown: https://brenebrown.com/

1:59 Eun Me Ahn https://www.facebook.com/159project/

The Festival of Audacious Women: Do what you always wished you dared https://festival.audaciouswomen.scot/

Hannah Gadsby https://www.youtube.com/watch?v=87qLWFZManA

Robin Morgan https://www.ted.com/talks/robin_morgan_4_powerful_poems_about_parkinson_s_and_growing_older?language=en

Mugen Taiko:

https://www.taiko.co.uk

About the Author

Alison Williams is an artist, writer and specialist in the practice and theory of creativity.

Alison's art practice draws on the relationship between spirit and the natural world, reflecting on what it means to be human, to be fully alive. She believes passionately in taking responsibility for her own life, in learning to love and care about others without wanting to take care of them.

Alison's spiritual journey with her Teachers, WindEagle and RainbowHawk, began in 1999 and continues to this day.

Born in Edinburgh, Scotland, she studied sculpture at Reading University. She lived in London and France, and co-founded a glass business whose clients included Paul McCartney and Freddie Mercury. Moving back to Scotland, Alison became what she calls "a late-onset academic" gaining a PhD in how physical space affects creativity in the workplace.

She is co-editor of BITE: Recipes for remarkable research and EqualBITE: Gender equality in higher education, two influential books that break the mould of academic publishing.

Contact Alison at her website www.wildingwomen.com

Printed in Great Britain
by Amazon

13144298R00154